Richard,

THE
FREEDOM
OF
CONSTRAINTS

With Gratitude !!!

Darren

THE
FREEDOM
OF
CONSTRAINTS

TURN OBSTACLES INTO OPPORTUNITY

DARCY VERHUN
FEATURING THE TALENTS OF THE MARSHALL GOLDSMITH 100 COACHES

THE FREEDOM OF CONSTRAINTS
Turn Obstacles Into Opportunity

Design Richard Sheinaus
Illustrations and Cover Concept John Halliday
Copyeditor Susan Rooks

ISBN #978-1-7778158-2-0 paperback
ISBN #978-1-7778158-1-3 hardcover
ISBN #978-1-7778158-0-6 ebook

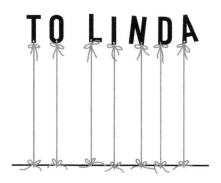

Table of Contents

Bright Future

Afterword

Introduction to Authors

"Life is really easy to talk – Life is really hard to do."
— Marshall Goldsmith

A few years ago, as Marshall Goldsmith turned 70 years old, he came up with the idea of "paying it forward" by teaching a group of people everything he learned over the years. His thinking included that as part of participating, each person needed to agree to also "pay it forward" when it was their time. Initially he thought that fifteen people would compose the group, but much to his surprise, tens of thousands put their name forward so it quickly grew to one hundred. Hence the name, Marshall Goldsmith 100 Coaches.

Marshall Goldsmith 100 Coaches is an organization that brings together many of the world's leading executive coaches, top business thinkers, retired CEOs, bestselling authors, and accomplished leaders – all with the common purpose of making good executives even better. These talented individuals are some of the top people in their fields. They represent leaders in their own worlds with a diversity of interests that relate to the topic of coaching and leadership. The Marshall Goldsmith 100 Coaches biographies can be found at www.100coaches.com.

This book is composed of essays from thirty of the Marshall Goldsmith 100 Coaches.

Our intent is to leave you with personal insights from our experience to help you to thrive in whatever challenges you may face. You can read this from cover to cover, selecting chapters based on the title or author, or picking from the themes and digging right in. Hopefully, what you learn will cause you to change in a way that is positive for you and your aspirations.

Introduction

By Darcy Verhun, *President at FYidoctors*

"So often in life, things that you regard as an impediment turn out to be great, good fortune."
— Ruth Bader Ginsburg

When industrial designer Ayse Birsel said to me that "...constraints will set you free...," I was puzzled. I had never thought of a constraint as an enabler before, so I pressed her to tell me more. Ayse went on to share that one of her early projects as a designer was with Herman Miller. She was to design a new system to be called Resolve, where the constraint was having to cut the cost of the company's lowest-cost office system (the Action Office Panel System) by 50 percent. The lower-cost requirement actually proved to be the spark for revolutionary thinking in her design work, and the result was a multi-award-winning office system. She told me she looked to nature for ideas that could be produced inexpensively but still provide the quality and style that Herman Miller was known for. For instance, she saw that honeycombs had high structural stability, so she used similar 120° angles. And she found ways to use smart materials in an honest manner while reducing the number of components. These became the cornerstones of the innovative thinking that resulted in Resolve.

"Leaning into the constraint and embracing it shifts your perspective to thinking positively about it, as an advantage. This optimism drives your creativity vs. sucking up the creative energy."
— Ayse Birsel, *Co-founder of Birsel + Seck, author of Design the Life You Love*

How many of us view boundaries or limitations as an advantage? I'm guessing, like me, very few. The very definition of a constraint seems to contradict this thinking.

Definition of *constraint* | noun

a: the act of constraining

b: the state of being checked, restricted, or compelled to avoid or perform some action

c: a constraining condition, agency, or force

— Merriam-Webster

None of the above definitions suggest that a constraint could be positive or an enabler of creativity. Yet what changes in our lives would we make if we recognized constraints and cherished them as enabling gifts? Perhaps that's a strange question to ask or even see meaning in, so let me expand. I had the pleasure of hearing Harry Kraemer, professor of leadership at Northwestern University, speak about life and leadership. He asked the group of us a question I believe he has considered deeply over his life. The question was, "What is 168?" No one seemed to know the answer. It turns out it is the number of hours in a week. He explained, "It is a constraint and a gift at the same time."

Recognizing that our time is finite creates an opportunity to use it as a precious resource. Knowing how much time we have forces choices about what we do, thereby eliminating surprises. Making conscious choices with our time – and placing chips on things that align with who and what we care about along with our hopes and aspirations – strengthens relationships and creates innovation, opportunity, growth, and learning. Treating our time as finite and then making decisions about what we do and how we use and invest our time allows us the best possibility of being who we aspire to be and shows others what we care about through our actions.

The constraint of time and how it is used frees us to view things through the lens of what is realistic to achieve, given the time invested.

I believe Harry when he said, "Either you figure out what you will stop doing or you will be surprised." Most people never consider how they are spending their time. Viewing it as finite can set us free to use it for what truly matters.

In this book, accomplished leaders, coaches, and designers share their reactions to constraints. From a retired Brigadier General to one of the world's top executive coaches to acclaimed authors, and from successful leaders to one of the world's foremost thinkers on brand, the coaches and leaders in this book will share their thinking, teach insights, share their perspectives, and regale us with stories.

This book has been created during a period when the entire world is experiencing a collective constraint, the global pandemic created by COVID-19. Our ambition with the words that follow is to inspire people – you particularly – to see constraints as opportunities. The pandemic has caused unprecedented pain and suffering, but the limitations imposed by the pandemic can and are creating possibilities. Hopefully, within the constraints of this volume and the unique chapters from each of the contributors, you'll find the innovation and insight you need to turn your own constraints into opportunities you would not otherwise have imagined.

Perhaps you will find the keys to unlock otherwise hidden opportunities, see hope, and lever your reality to achieve your aspirations. My hope is that we have a positive impact beyond our individual reach, to combine our voices in a way that amplifies our message and insights, and to do so in a way that is of value to all.

So, as you prepare to dive in, I share my final thought: Cherish the constraints you face and embrace them to unlock unseen opportunities.

Life Shapes
Who We Are and
Who We
May Become

n the stories that are shared in the following essays, we learn from a group of authors who dealt with significant life challenges. These stories share vulnerability while providing insights into the authors' life journeys and how they adapted and thrived. The lessons: Discovering what is truly important to you will allow you to leverage your past experiences to advantage; understanding how the power of the choices you make can be used to free yourself to be who you aspire to be and achieve your goals; and knowing that relentless commitment separates those who just dream from those who achieve.

Boundaries Reveal Who We Are
How Constraints Can Guide You to Make Your Best Contribution to the World

By Connie Dieken, *Influence 360° Founder, Strategic Advisor, Bestselling Author,* Hall of Fame Broadcaster

"The more constraints one imposes, the more one frees one's self."
— Igor Stravinsky

We've all heard the expression that your past can come back to haunt you. During the pandemic, I discovered the reverse lesson: that your past can return to reveal a compelling future—not just for you, but for others.

My story starts in a tiny town in rural USA—a community so small that people from the boonies might call it the sticks. My dad, like most men in town, worked all of his life in the glass factory that anchored the town. My mom was the town nurse. In my younger years, I thought my humble upbringing was a constraint—but turns out, it was an advantage. We'll get to that later.

I grew up surrounded by good people with strong values: Do the right thing, be thoughtful, and put others' needs before your own. In high school, a teacher needed to enter a student in the Future Business Leaders of America public speaking competition, so she signed me up. Somehow, against all odds, this small-town girl with absolutely no business savvy won contest after contest and made it to the national championship, which led to a college scholarship. Only a small fraction of my classmates went to college, so this was big news.

Spurred by my initial public speaking triumph, I joined the college PBS television station. Yes, unworldly as I was, I connected public speaking with the Public Broadcasting Service. Between classes and waitressing shifts to pay for room and board, I spent nearly every day at the station writing copy for the on-air staff, honing my skills. One day, the station's talk show host called in sick, and they needed someone in the office to pinch-hit on-air. Suddenly, it was show time!

That led to more on-air work. I built a broadcasting demo reel, and upon graduation, I caught the eye of ABC News New York where I was awarded a Fellowship. In short order, this nobody from the middle of nowhere had launched a career at the top of the television industry. Shortly after, a head-hunter from NBC recruited me away and fast-tracked me to become a network newswoman.

We're talking a real "pinch me, is this real?" opportunity here.

This is where I veered off script a bit. As I settled into my first anchor-woman assignment at a network-owned station in the Midwest, I fell in love, married, and had two beautiful children. I'd spend mornings and early afternoons with my family and then head to the station to write and deliver the evening and late-night news.

Next came a values clash—the first boundary.

Once my children reached school age, I wanted to be present for homework and after-school activities, which meant that I'd need to shift my work schedule to daytime broadcasts.

Let's just say the conversation with the TV station's management team wasn't well received. With its higher visibility and ratings, the evening news brought the station much higher advertising revenue, and that's where they wanted me.

Management wouldn't budge. I was boxed in. So, I resigned.

"You'll regret this decision for the rest of your life," my former boss said. "No one walks away from this opportunity." "With all due respect, sir," I replied, "the only thing I'd regret is if I didn't follow my values and raise my children to the best of my ability."

And with that, I swiftly slid down the corporate ladder.

After a mandatory noncompete period, I started a new role with family-friendly hours as co-host of a morning talk show at a television station across town. As the oldest, most established talk show in America, this live show was a magnet for compelling guests like CEOs, bestselling authors, and global celebrities. I loved researching and interviewing influential people. It was a livewire act, and it felt great to connect the dots between high-profile leaders' insights and our audience's needs.

After a few years, the broadcasting industry changed dramatically. Along came the "live feed," which meant that savvy PR teams plopped their clients—our highest-profile guests—in a central studio for efficiency, doing interviews round-robin style rather than flying them to studios like ours. This meant bye-bye deep conversations and hello generic talking points.

The station's management didn't think this was the best use of my skills, and I understood. They called a meeting to say they wanted to move me to the evening news broadcasts. You know, the predictably profitable time slot.

But I stood firm. I couldn't be away from my kids in the evenings—parenting was more important to me than anything in the world.

This time the stakes were even higher. I was now a single mother with a mortgage, on her own. Walking away would mean that I had no income to support us.

If you're like most people, you see this as a constraint. I didn't want my work shift to conflict with my children's schedule, and I didn't want to take a job in another city because I wanted my kids to grow up in their hometown. After a few sleepless nights and sphincter-tightening moments, I decided to walk away. Again. But I'd use this as an opportunity to build a new career that wouldn't be constrained by someone else's idea of an ideal work schedule.

I used my deep curiosity about what makes leaders influential and launched a business, *The Influence Lab*. That was 20 years ago and since that time, I've led a major research study on leadership influence, designed a psychometric tool to measure it, written two bestselling books on the subject, and coached thousands of executives at the world's biggest brands on how to influence positive change.

I believe this is the role I was born to fill all along.

Once my children were grown, I began traveling the globe coaching CEOs in person and delivering keynote speeches. The same small-town girl who hadn't stepped on an airplane until she was 18 was now a jetsetter, flying from Silicon Valley to South America, from the Midwest to the Middle East.

In March of 2020, I was scheduled to fly to conferences in Bahrain and Budapest. Then came COVID. With the onset of the pandemic, conferences and business travel came to a screeching halt. And rightfully so. We all needed boundaries to keep each other safe.

But it's also true that many of us were constraining our thinking about the future of our businesses pre-pandemic and didn't realize it. The pandemic revealed new ways to influence positive change faster, more completely, and for the long term.

With travel out of the question and clients' needs even more urgent, I retooled. I drew upon my television background and with the help of a digital team, built a broadcasting studio in my home that allowed me to connect with my clients' needs, unconstrained by travel or time.

And with that, COVID's "constraints" became an edge. I could now respond to clients anywhere, anytime.

Here are a few lessons I'd like to share about how boundaries can bring you full circle to where you are meant to be:

Constraints are often an advantage in disguise

When the pandemic hit, I began to adjust my mindset: What could be *done better* virtually than in person?

In my transition from newswoman to leadership advisor, I learned the difference between *broadcasting* and *narrowcasting*. We *broadcast* to a large, diverse audience; we *narrowcast* to a specific audience.

Executive coaching and small-group workshops can be incredibly impactful *narrowcasts* if you know how to set them up effectively, which my broadcasting background gave me the edge to do.

What past experiences and expertise can you draw upon when faced with a constraint? How can it be an advantage? What comes naturally to you may be just the edge that your new conditions call for.

Constraints eliminate second-guessing

This was a big lesson for me. There was no time for second-guessing during the pandemic. Speed was of the essence. I learned to forget perfection and think excellence to get things up and running. Narrowing my focus helped me leap ahead.

Many business projects have a better chance of success when boundaries are defined. Turns out this is a lot like parenting and live TV broadcasts. So, define the boundaries, accept them, and work within them.

Are you conditioned to hold back until you think things are perfect? Do you habitually second-guess your decisions? Forget it. Get moving, narrow your focus, and make a contribution. In our new world, speed trumps perfection.

Constraints separate the talkers from the doers

Some people see constraints as frustrating roadblocks. They complain about imperfect conditions and use them as excuses for why they can't perform at their highest level.

Others see constraints as challenges. They reframe them, not blame them—and these are the people who excel during crises.

The pandemic exposed the talkers and the doers: those who talk a good game but don't deliver and those who, given the ball, run with it and shape positive change.

For example, a chief technology officer whom I coach used the pandemic to launch a digital transformation at his company. He guided his team through game-changing moves that had been tabled before the pandemic. He ran with the opportunity, and as a result, the CTO's initiatives fundamentally changed the future of the organization, leading to millions in revenue growth.

Who are you surrounding yourself with—talkers or doers? Use these revelations to align with the doers and give them the ability to reveal what they can do.

Constraints can spark deeper commitment

I advised many of the CEOs whom I coach to send frequent, personal video messages to their workforces. More important, I asked them to request 30-second videos in response from employees who wanted to share a concern or ask a question.

My clients were shocked at how many responses they received. The responses unearthed confusion and resistance from deep within their ranks, allowing the leaders to make quick changes and help their employees move from resistance to resilience, from compliance to commitment.

Are you hearing from enough voices? Use every opportunity to ensure that you're bringing resistance to the surface, and give your team the gift of mutual commitment.

Constraints can reshape your leadership influence

As a social scientist, my team's research focuses on how leaders attempt to change resistant stakeholders' minds. Our 20-year study revealed that the most common reason why leaders fail to influence positive change is because they're persuasive, but not influential.

What's the difference between persuasion and influence? Sustainability. Persuasion focuses on stopgap, short-term decisions. The trap of persuasion is that you're susceptible to the next act of persuasion that comes along. Influence, on the other hand, is long term. Influential leaders connect the dots between the here-and-now and the possibilities of the future that lead to lasting change.

And this is where the pandemic has handed us a once-in-a-lifetime gift. The many constraints the pandemic imposed have given leaders the chance to redefine their organizations and their leadership. It's a rare chance to unify people, elevate ideas into actions, and shape the future.

Do you use constraints to persuade one-off actions? Instead, think big picture: Use them to rethink, retool, and reveal a better path forward.

Today, I find myself in a *Back to the Future* world. I realize now that I'm still a broadcaster. Truth is, we're all broadcasters in a digital world. The key is to narrowcast the right message to the right audience at the right time.

And it turns out that my small-town naiveté was an edge because I didn't constrain myself. I wasn't afraid to start at the top because I wasn't reined in by fear. I didn't know what I didn't know.

Living your values is never a constraint—it's a remarkably positive boundary that can set you free to make your best contribution to the world.

I hope that whatever challenges or constraints may throw you off-center in the future will also reveal your strengths—and guide you to the very spot where you were meant to be all along.

__Connie Dieken, CSP, CPAE__, is the founder of The Influence Lab®. Named the world's #1 Executive Communication Coach by The Global Gurus® organization, she guides C-level leaders at the world's biggest brands to influence positive change. The bestselling author of two books, "Talk Less, Say More" and "Become the Real Deal," Connie has also been honored with five Emmy Awards® and been inducted into the Radio/TV Broadcasters Hall of Fame® and the Speakers Hall of Fame®.

www.ConnieDieken.com

I am the Problem

By Laura Gassner Otting, *Chief Catalyzing Officer, Limitless Possibility*

"The way I see it, if you want the rainbow, you gotta put up with the rain."
— Dolly Parton

As a bit of background, I work as an author and a professional keynote speaker. COVID-19 decimated the events industry. No events, no speaking. No speaking, no income.

COVID-19 killed my business.

Except, it wasn't COVID-19's fault. It was mine.

For the first two months of the pandemic, I complained, whined, and cried to anyone who would listen that COVID-19 was the problem. COVID-19 was stopping me from running my business. COVID-19 was not letting me get on planes and stages. COVID-19 was getting in between me and the speaking business that I spent the years building.

"It's all the fault of COVID-19."

This frustration came out in many forms. Maybe I got political: It's the fault of all those politicians who didn't respond correctly, choosing political expediency over science. Maybe I got personal: It's the fault of all those neighbors who didn't wash their hands or wear a mask or stay home when they were first coughing, choosing immediate, personal gratification over staying home for the common good. Maybe (okay, certainly) I got judgy: It's the fault of all those selfish people who insisted on flying, cruising, and spring-breaking, as chaos and confusion reigned.

It didn't change the outcome: My business tanked, and I wanted someone to blame.

So, I did. I blamed everyone else. But the truth is that it wasn't their fault; it was mine.

I had to realize that I was the problem.

In the midst of my rage of a two-month-long pity party in which I gained the "COVID-15" as I mainlined s'more after s'more after s'more melted over the fire of the burning ashes of a speaking business that was finally gaining warp speed momentum, I had a moment of clarity: COVID-19 wasn't stopping me from doing what I love, with people I love, helping them get unstuck and live limitless lives. I was stopping myself.

I was stopping myself because I believed that the only way to do it was how I've always done it.

I was stopping myself because I assumed that stages and audiences only came in one form.

I was stopping myself because I decided — without any basis in fact — that I couldn't possibly reach an audience bigger than the dream gigs with 5,000 people, who were, of course, hanging on my every word, and without those audiences, I couldn't make an impact.

In April of 2019, I published a book entitled *Limitless: How to Ignore Everybody, Carve Your Own Path, and Live Your Best Life*. It is based on 20 years of work in executive search during which time I interviewed thousands of leaders in bowel-shaking moments of career shift, and stewarded hundreds of clients through earth-shaking moments of organizational disruption. I was struck during my time in executive search that, over and over, I was asked to call the most successful people on the planet and recruit them away on my client's behalf. But what made this job easier was the fact that, over and over, despite all this success, the people I was calling weren't very happy.

We are all carrying around this scorecard in our back pockets, whether we realize it or not, and regardless of whether or not we know where we got it, and that scorecard is the one that tells us exactly what success is supposed to look like. It's everybody else's version of everybody else's success. But, what if everybody else's version of everybody else's success doesn't equal our own personal happiness?

Here is the meta-moment realization that the pandemic unlocked for me: I was limiting myself by defining success in the way that it had historically been defined in my profession, by everybody else, for everybody else. And I was either too distracted, too anxious, too uncertain, or just too busy hoarding toilet paper to get creative.

Each of us does the work that we do because there is a specific problem that we would like to solve. What if we could completely reimagine the way that we solved that problem differently, through a different medium or framework or rubric or methodology? What if we could redefine our "stage" and expand it well beyond what we thought was a "big audience" heretofore? What if we could show up in new and different ways that augmented what makes us special, so that we could be better for those people we love and the causes we hold dear?

The problem we are trying to solve isn't COVID-19. We've got scientists and healthcare professionals for that. The problem we are trying to solve is the problem that we dedicated our work to before we'd ever even heard about the virus, the problem we are trying to solve that still exists.

The problem now is that our distractions, our anxiety, our uncertainty (and maybe even that nagging toilet paper problem) are getting in the way.

My problem wasn't that COVID-19 tanked my business. My problem was that I was so distracted thinking COVID-19 was the problem that I didn't realize that the problem was my own lack of clarity and creativity.

I was the problem, and there was no escaping it.

COVID-19 upended the way we do our work, the way we organize our communities, the way we lead our teams. It's been difficult, but it's also opened up new possibilities.

There has never been a time where access to other people's minds, hearts, and wallets has been so democratized. No one and nothing is stopping you or me from showing up and providing solutions but us and our preconceived notions of what our "stages" should look like, what our success should look like. There is a whole new carnival in town with all sorts of new rides, and the price of entry for me was simply a webcam and an internet connection.

That means asking ourselves better questions, so that we might come up with better answers.

What is the calling you want to serve?

What is the work you can do to connect to that calling?

What is the most effective medium through which you can do so?

The answer to those questions is nothing but clarity.

The answer to those questions is nothing but creativity.

The answer to those questions is nothing but limitless possibility.

This is my path forward.

What's yours?

Laura Gassner Otting is an executive coach, keynote speaker, and the Washington Post Bestselling Author of "Limitless: How to Ignore Everybody," "Carve Your Own Path," and "Live Your Best Life." She was voted the #2 Start Up Coach in the World and the #10 Top Motivational Speaker in the World by Global Gurus. She is a frequent guest expert on Good Morning, America and the Today show.

https://www.linkedin.com/in/heylgo/ www.LauraGassnerOtting.com

Who Shows Up?
Unexpected Visitors. Welcomed Gifts.

By Alex Lazarus, *Behaviour Change Scientist | Founder of Lazarus & Maverick*

"Omnia mea mecum porto. All that is mine I carry with me."
 — Cicero

E
astern Europe. Summer 1991.
    On a beautiful summer evening, when I was a teenager on a school
    break, our family apartment atop a jungle of concrete '70s high-
rises ceased to exist as I knew it. And so did my life.

Minutes earlier, I was standing outside our front door with a heavy heart and a key in my hand. Steeped in the sounds of communal life echoing through the infinite staircase, I gathered that this was probably a legitimate moment to fall apart. The very idea made me feel nauseous, so I decided to get in fast and fall apart later.

As I entered our apartment, it looked burgled. There were clothes scattered everywhere, drawers left open, curtains slammed by the balcony door wriggling away on the other side. Squinting from the sunset painting the rooms orange, I moved into the lounge and sat down. Looking through dust particles floating in the stream of light, taking it moment by moment, hit me hard. "So that's what the end of a family looks like."

My wonderful mother and the only person I lived with was now gone. Having packed her suitcase frantically at the last minute, she had boarded a plane for the first time in her life just a few hours earlier. The path leading up to our goodbye at the departure gate stretched in years of preparations, so why was I in disbelief? A few years earlier, the fall of Communism and the tearing down of the Berlin Wall gave us signs that life would change. And that day, after years of living behind the Iron Curtain, she was somewhere in the airspace crossing over to the West.

Knowing that it could be years rather than weeks before I would see her again, I choked back the tears and amused myself by thinking that at least she got a window seat. And what a view that must be! The truth of how I truly felt, though, was irrefutable.

I was now entirely on my own.

"The universe is not outside of you. Look inside yourself; everything that you want, you already are."
    — *Rumi*

What followed next taught me that strange and great things can happen at the intersection of emptiness and ending. With tears on standby and my falling apart a moment away, it dawned on me that I had a choice. I could cry, or I could tidy up.

In that moment, jolted out of stillness, parts of me I never knew existed showed up to offer support. While one part of me was broken, another came to the rescue. The weaker I felt, the stronger I grew. My vulnerable self ached to cry over getting through life alone, but my pragmatic self remained unperturbed; she saw things in simple terms. "Every moment that's about to happen is irreversible. You have the power to choose what you do and whom you become," said the voice.

Deep down, I knew it was true, but uncertainty has a cunning way to muzzle the power of mind over matter. What about neighbours, teachers, and all who would be interested in my living situation? Would I be allowed to live at home alone? Will I end up in a depressing high school dorm for kids out of town? With a hint of rebellion, my creative self shrugged it off. "You'll figure it out. Life is a game. Play it." Again, easier said than done. To offer a different perspective, my positive self added, "When it gets tough, let joy in to let joy win!" And my future self beamed a message from the time to come that since life was looking pretty good over there, there really was no point in falling apart just yet, so I might as well tidy up.

Right there, this party of selves, like good fairies, brought gifts of timeless insights and wisdom granted by my conscious and unconscious heritage of those before me and those in my future. Discovering the universe of my inner selves was essentially discovering the role of one's inner voice and the kind of imagination that, when presented with a void, gets vibrant, comes alive, and offers choices.

Stirred by crisis and let loose by constraint, imagination would serve as my only resource that made something out of nothing, my insurance against shyness, fear, or lack of skills.

Having no parental supervision and no chance of ever being told off again, I had to quickly get acquainted with both my positive and my destructive potential.

While I might have fallen flat on my face quite a few times in the challenging years that ensued, a quick self-check saved me from trouble on the whole. I got better at stopping, pausing, and paying attention to which part of me was showing up in moments that mattered.

Was I at the mercy of my inner critic ranting? Or was I in luck with my kind self arising?

Whose behaviour, legacy, and future was I allowing myself to be bound to?

And finally, what could my future self see that I could not yet see?

"There is no greater agony than bearing an untold story inside you."
— *Maya Angelou*

Six years later. London. 1997.

As a foreigner who lived on the wrong side of the Cold War, I was deemed unemployable, or employable for the "cash in hand" black market only. While anxious about how I would jump over the immigrant label and other uncomfortable assumptions, I was nevertheless undeterred. Possibility and impossibility went hand in hand, and the tension between them was always present.

David Bowie once said, "Even though I was very shy, I found I could get onstage if I had a new identity." For me, it was future self who presented that anchor, although dreaming her up felt audacious and out of bounds at the best of times. Unlike me, my future self was free; she was a global citizen, an artist, a thinker, a professional, a leader, an activist, a human making a difference in the world. However, over time, the more I tuned in to her for guidance, the more believable she became, giving me faith that my untold story was worth fighting for.

My future self was watchful and cheering me on. She was there for me when I turned up a mess and half an hour late at the house of Richard Branson, the billionaire founder of Virgin, for a job interview beyond my wildest dreams. Here I was, soaked to the skin, mascara blasted off my face by strong gales and torrential rain, staring at Branson's beautiful white Victorian townhouse. Instead of practicing my interview lines, I was cursing myself for refusing to carry an umbrella. How could I be so unwise, so un-streetwise and unworldly to refuse to believe that I would get rained on in London one day?

Well, today was that day!

While my pragmatic self, dumbfounded and speechless, tut-tutted "No comment," the proud and future selves were now at war:

Proud Self: *"You're late. Disgraceful. Go home!"*

Future Self: *"Walk up and ring that bell now."*

Proud Self: *"Save yourself embarrassment!"*

Future Self: *"Knock on that door. The longer you stand there, the later it gets."*

Proud Self: *"You blew it."*

As the shouting match continued, I burst out crying and walked away. With each step, my future seemed foggier. By the time I got back to Holland Park station, however, the rain had stopped, and I stopped. What should I do? I closed my eyes, heart pounding, and I listened to my soul; I needed to unearth whatever wisdom I could excavate. I sensed an unfinished business and an unheard voice. I tuned in to it deeply.

"It's now or never. It's that simple." My future self showed up and said, "Incredible things don't happen on incredible days. They happen when least expected." There is hope. Giving myself a second chance, I turned back and ran for dear life across the street. I sprinted down

Holland Park, past all the houses yet again and up to Branson's gate. Now, not only soaking wet, but completely out of breath and forty minutes late, I rang the bell.

And I got the job.

"Sweet are the uses of adversity."
     — Shakespeare

It is possibly the greatest irony of life that the worst day of my childhood and the isolation and constraints of Communism in which I grew up resulted in the best life lessons, which sustain me to this day:

Being human is complex – Pablo Neruda once said, "When everything seems to be set to show me off as a man of intelligence, the fool I keep concealed on my person takes over my talk and occupies my mouth." Indeed, being human is paradoxical in nature. We are complex, beautiful, messy, disgraceful, winning, losing, desiring, regretting, loving, hating, incredible creatures. Recognising this was key to accepting myself as I was. Rather than perfection, I aimed for progress.

There is always a choice – As Sartre, the French philosopher said, "We are our choices." Unlike involuntary acts like breathing or reflexes, I learnt to own the power of choice and intention. Whether you make a choice or don't, it's still a decision.

Keep the big picture in mind – When in the grip of a crisis, it's easy to allow it to engulf our entire sense of existence. What helped me in adversity was taking a step back and noticing how that moment in time related to the big picture of my life.

While admitting that the challenges were real, recognising that they were temporary in nature strengthened my resilience and the resolve to get through the worst.

Courage versus competence and confidence – For a while, unpredictability and constraints were the only constants in my life. As I lacked skills or experience, competence and confidence were not my friends. Instead, I relied on tuning in to my courageous self to bridge difficult situations. In crises, courage helped me gain experience, and experience, in turn, fuelled competency and confidence, but not the other way round.

"The best way to predict the future is to create it."
— *Peter F. Drucker*

Closing thoughts

Spring 2021.

Little did I know that the summer of 1991 would lead to a lifelong interest in leadership and transformation, for which I was awarded a distinction for research on identity as a resource for change, and a Master of Science degree in Coaching and Behavioural Change. Those early lessons also led to a career in media and TV for global brands including Virgin, Fox, and Disney, which I left as Marketing Director with a mission to develop exceptional leadership capabilities around the world that would improve the lives of others.

Subsequently, I founded Lazarus & Maverick leadership consultancy, where with a team of experts in behavioural change and coaching, we help clients like Spotify, Viacom, AIG, KPMG, Qualcomm, and others to succeed and to build their own powerful future story.

When the pandemic struck, those lessons proved indispensable again. There were bright days; there were dark days.

Despite uncertainty, I leaned on courage rather than confidence and kept the bigger picture in mind when making investments to our infrastructure, to support clients virtually. When the year ended, we couldn't believe that we helped over 10,000 people across multiple time zones. Curious to understand traits of exceptional future leaders of the changing world, we also conducted a global research study with Global Leaders in Law and Morrison & Foerster.

Above all, I stayed close to my family, wonderful colleagues, and clients, learning how to deal with complexity, psychology of change, resilience, and ambiguity.

As the most popular insight for many was that getting through adversity depends on how we engage with all kinds of inner critics and inner guides taking up residency in our own mind, I would like to leave the reader with some questions:

Which one of your voices shows up the most for you in times of crisis?

Which one will you influence to become your torch bearer?

What can your future self see that you cannot yet see?

Alex is the founder of Lazarus & Maverick, a global leadership consultancy. Alex is the author of "Leading with Influence" Research Report, named as one of the Most Influential Thought Leaders to Follow in 2021 (peopleHum), shortlisted International Coach of the Year, and a recipient of the Gold Award by the Marketing Agencies Association Worldwide. She is a happy mum, a so-so snowboarder and a good enough musician. She still refuses to carry an umbrella.

www.lazarusandmaverick.co.uk

You Can't Control What Happens.
You Can Control What You Do and The Questions You Ask.

By Alisa Cohn, *#1 Startup Coach in the World – Thinkers50*

"If you don't like something, change it. If you can't change it, change your attitude."
— Maya Angelou

n the 2001 documentary of Ram Das, the author and Buddhist spiritual teacher talks about his experience of having his stroke in 1997. "I didn't have a single spiritual thought," he said. "It was a test. And I flunked the test." Ram Das would have thought he was spiritual enough to hold his stroke in an enlightened state, but instead he found himself lonely and self-pitying. "I could see I had more work to do."

I could say the same for my initial reaction to the pandemic. I'm a coach, for Pete's sake! I've done a lot of self-development. I work with my clients to accept what is and to find the power in seeing what they can do, rather than moan about their circumstances. I've activated this in my own life as well, building my business from scratch, working out with heavy weights to make my body strong, taking on a meditation practice to enhance my spiritual life.

But on March 13, 2020, when I realized that the pandemic was more than just a passing inconvenience, there is no other way to put it: I flunked this test. I yelled. I cried. I fought against every moment.

Then, slowly, perspective took over, and I was able to take stock.

Although I was off my game, to say the least, I heard one small voice in my head loud and clear: Do not waste this time. So, imperfectly, I took actions. Now, just about a year later, I see that the constraints of the pandemic led me to one of the most fruitful creative spurts of my life.

Commitment has power

The most significant thing I did in March was let in that little voice that told me: Do not waste this time. It was tempting – very – to allow my self-pitying scared self take over. It would have been easy to watch a lot of movies and eat a lot of carbs.

And I would not have been the only one to do so.

But I didn't. I committed myself to using this time in a way that, when looking back, I would feel proud. I thought a lot about what would make me feel that way, and two clear answers emerged.

Take a step forward on writing the book you said you wanted to.

Be more deliberate in how you use your time and stop procrastinating.

Those were my commitments. Both of these were very uncomfortable for me – there's a reason I had never worked through my block in writing a book! I procrastinated, so that I wouldn't have to feel the discomfort of uncertainty. But, I found, as did the poet Johann Wolfgang von Goethe in the 1700s: "At the moment of commitment the entire universe conspires to assist you."

Here's a question for you to consider: What will you commit to so that your future self will applaud you?

Set internal deadlines

So I got to work. I called a few wise friends to get their help with my internal state (what was in the way of my writing this book?), and I called up a few more to hold me accountable. I organized notecards; I wrote and then rewrote my table of contents. I sketched out the interviews I wanted to do and wrote the introduction. I eradicated moments of procrastination. I set up a clear schedule and made rules for myself about what I would do instead when tempted to put things off.

I made it a game and gave myself little deadlines to accomplish certain things. To my surprise, I found myself sprinting to meet the deadlines. Ah, I see. When I create my own constraints, I'm the author of my circumstances.

Not only that, but as the late winter turned into spring, people began to complain about the monotony. It was *Groundhog Day*, everyone said. Not to me. I had progress to make. I knew what I had to get done by Friday, and I knew what a two-week schedule looked like. It turns out that every day doesn't feel the same when you have progressive deliverables.

After a few months of this, I had written many more articles for *Harvard Business Review, Inc.*, and *Forbes* than in all of the prior year. And, I had myself a book contract (with an external deadline, by the way).

So here is a tactical question: What is a clear milestone that will help drive you?

Releasing control gives birth to creativity

I (and everyone I knew) had lived with a sense that you can count on your life being more or less the same, and changes come when you decide to make them.

No more. The pandemic robbed me of having the illusion of control. I was in deep mourning for my past life – the life I had built in NYC, the life I loved. It was also the life I had counted on. I knew where I was headed to and where I was in that process, and I knew how to keep score. But there was another side to that certainty. I had been ignoring some of the passions that would feed my spirit.

A new voice inside of me asked this: "What are you waiting for?" For years I had been putting off creative pursuits. Yes, I had invested in Broadway shows over the past few years, but in my heart I wanted to be a performer. I put off exploring that until – well, until some day in the future.

For no reason except for fun, I decided to create a music video. I called up a friend for help, and he talked me into doing a rap music video we created together, called "The Work Is in You." It was super uncomfortable. It was also incredibly rewarding. I knew I needed more music in my life, and now I had this little experience. Next, I found a piano and started taking lessons.

The pandemic freed me up to do something just for myself.

So, a question for you: What are you waiting for?

Vulnerability equals connection

One of the executive teams I work with had a meeting on video three days after New York shut down. We were alert, solemn. The CEO started the meeting with everyone just sharing a few words about how they were. When my turn came, nobody was more surprised than I was to find myself getting weepy. It took me longer than I would have thought to compose myself, which I did, and then we had our meeting.

After that session, several of the executives reached out to me to offer me comfort, which was nice, and thanks, which was surprising. "When you teared up, you gave all of us permission to not be fully ok," the CEO emailed me. "I don't know if you realized it but even on the video the energy shifted. I think that was the moment we all got connected. We needed that."

Sometimes my job as a coach is to be strong for others. But in that moment, it was to model how you can be human as well as resolute.

So a good question to ask is: Where do you need to take the risk to show your true self a little more?

Renew yourself

It's been a long year. The effects of the pandemic are not going to go away overnight. And some of the ways we typically renew ourselves may not be available. I mourn the events I didn't get to go to this year, which are always so regenerating: Renaissance Weekend – a multi-genera-tional, multi-discipline gathering of incredibly interesting people where we talk about our lives and let down our guards. TED – a fascinating collection of the world's top minds in varied fields where we discuss breakthrough ideas together.

Change of scenery is always restorative – but not this year. Seeing friends from out of town rejuvenates the soul – and will have to wait.

It's easy to focus on the things you can't do, but again creative lives on the flip-side: What can you do to regenerate yourself in a time that you need it more than ever? What I came up with for myself is a set of things that I can do in combination. Now that I'm living in the suburbs, I'm finding that walking among the trees, grass, and birds is pretty meditative. I can combine walking with listening to fascinating podcasts, which bring the world to me, and with calls with friends, which let me keep connections with people. I'm creating my own regenerative curriculum to fuel my soul and my mind.

What can you do to sharpen your saw?

We are emerging from the pandemic, and one day this will be behind us. But what I hope for myself and for you is that we take away the value of the constraints that the pandemic forced on all of us.[1]

Named the #1 Startup Coach in the World by Thinkers50, **Alisa Cohn** *has been coaching startup founders to grow into world-class CEOs for 20 years. A one-time CFO, she was named the #1 "Global Guru" for startups. She has coached startups such as Venmo, Etsy, and The Wirecutter, and enterprise clients such as Dell, Google, Microsoft, and Bloomberg. Her articles have appeared in HBR, and Inc., and she has been featured as an expert on BBC World News and in The New York Times.*

Find out more about Alisa at AlisaCohn.com and follow her on Twitter @AlisaCohn. Download her "Questions to Spark Conversations" here: https://bit.ly/ACtableQhbr

[1] A version of this chapter originally appeared in Forbes.com

Constraint? Maybe Not.

By Beth Polish, *Thought Leader | Executive Coach | Trusted Advisor | CEO at Stretch Industries, LLC*

"Remember always that you not only have the right to be an individual, you have an obligation to be one."
— Eleanor Roosevelt

At my elementary school graduation, I won the Citizenship Award. We didn't have a valedictorian or salutatorian, but there was an award for the student in the graduating class who had gone above and beyond for the community. I was astonished that I'd won. My mom wasn't.

From the time I was old enough to have playdates, my mom had taught me what it meant to be a good guest and a good host. At its simplest, being a good guest meant playing whatever my host wanted to play, and being a good host meant playing whatever my guest wanted to play. Either way, I had to play with enthusiasm, because that was how I showed how much I appreciated their friendship – by supporting what they wanted. It was just good manners.

To a just-turned double-digit-aged girl, this made sense.

My mom's focus, as she would tell me later, was to make sure my brother and I were civilized – if we had good manners, then we could go anywhere. And that was the first step to being a good citizen – thinking about others first. So, to my mom, I got the award because I had extended that sense of responsibility toward others to my larger school community. My 10-year-old self was so excited and proud – the award meant so much to me – that I have yet to cash in the $25 bond that came with it! And it reinforced my mom's admonitions about what it means to be a good person.

Here's the thing, though. These teachings were more than simple constraints. Together, they put me in a box – one that didn't allow me much room to move around because they were binary – you were either a good guest or not, a good host or not. It was all or nothing; there were no shades of grey.

As I grew intellectually, I began to realize that the world is much bigger and way more nuanced than those simple formulations suggested. And in my college years, I had a couple of experiences that accelerated those new perceptions.

I went off to college at a relatively young age (I applied at 15 and started at 16) thinking I'd be a large-animal veterinarian. I loved animals, especially horses, and I was an avid rider. My original plan had been to go to riding school in England between high school and college, but I bumped up against another constraint – smart Jewish girls don't go away to riding school; they go to college and graduate school. So, I'd found a goal that would serve both needs – as a large-animal vet I could be a "professional" and be around horses. Thankfully, I learned early that being a veterinarian wasn't the right path for me, and I'd taken a course in anthropology that offered a better one.

Studying anthropology changed everything for me. I loved the idea of seeing the world through someone else's eyes and not judging what I saw. It taught me what it means to have real empathy, because I learned how to seek out the nuance, to understand what is real, and to see where the grey areas are, and how to be comfortable navigating in through those seemingly messy places. It was liberating. It let me see a way to be my mom's good citizen, only smarter and more impactful.

During my freshman year of college, I went to work for a friend of my father's, one of the first women to have a seat on the stock exchange. Sandra was strong and powerful. She had started out as a teacher but decided she didn't want her income and career constrained by others. Instead, she was going to live or die based on objective measures of her work. The route she chose was being a stockbroker, and she became a successful career woman in a man's business. She didn't think about playing by the existing rules (other than the regulatory ones); she focused on what mattered for her clients. And as my first real boss, she focused on what really mattered in mentoring me and teaching me what it meant to be a professional.

What she didn't care about was how I dressed for work. I knew enough to wear a dress, but at 17 I rebelled against things like stockings and sleeves, and that was okay with her. It was only later that I found out she was protecting me from the company's dress code for women. That was a constraint she thought could be navigated around, though she, herself, was always impeccably dressed. I learned many things from Sandra over those January term breaks, summers, and beyond; perhaps the most important one was not to accept the status quo as immutable, that some constraints fade to insignificance in the bigger picture.

With this broadening of my perspective, my way of liberating myself from my childhood constraint-box became to find work opportunities where breaking the rules and overcoming constraints carried the potential to build something new and valuable to a larger community. This started with my first corporate job out of college, working for the CTO of Dun & Bradstreet. George believed it was possible to deliver D&B credit reports via a computer voice-response system, that the constraint that said it had to be human-to-human to work was nearsighted. He was determined to deliver the verbal reports purely by computer, and that's what we did, not just for D&B but for all the companies they licensed our technology to.

It was an extraordinary experience, not only watching George navigating the global D&B ship – hugely risk-averse as the market leader in its area – into entirely new seas, but also learning how to figure out what constraints are real and what aren't on the route to building a disruptive (and very successful) new business.

After business school, I continued to find constraint-challenging positions, and with each one my leadership skills grew. iVillage was a pivotal one. As founding COO/CFO, I came to the company an already practiced user of a brand new thing called the World Wide Web, with first-hand knowledge of what was possible. This was in 1995, when the first user-friendly browsers were just coming out and there was no large consumer Internet yet.

My business school friends thought I was nuts to give up a secure job for some woman-focused Internet play – it was a given that women would remain no more than 25% of all Internet users, and women didn't really have buying power in the home. As the founding team, we didn't buy any of that. We saw those constraints as things of the past. Where others saw risk, we saw opportunity. In the end, iVillage was one of the key contributors to a changed narrative about women, money, and advertising that has fueled the Internet economy ever since.

I haven't stopped putting myself in situations where I can marry my anthropology-informed way of looking at things with an ability to see possibilities where others see roadblocks, where I can move boundaries so there is more freedom and a road to success, where I can lead people in creating something valuable for users, where I can swap out a constraint-driven mindset for a growth, forward-moving one. Where the power of story-telling ties it all together.

I got to do this in spades when I was hired by the Hearst Corporation to come up with a plan for a company-wide innovation group. My assignment was to develop the plan, present it to the CEO, and if he accepted it, to come on board to run the group. As I got going, talking to people throughout the company, I saw people who really wanted to be more innovative for the company but who, at the same time, told me all the reasons why it wouldn't work.

Perhaps because I hadn't grown up in the company, I saw the very real constraints they described not as roadblocks, but, more often than not, as company folklore to navigate. I have Bob, my advisor there, to thank for helping me see that sometimes you have to be patient and address constraints one at a time. Ultimately, the innovation group I created ended up being first about changing perceptions of what was possible. From there the business opportunities could flow.

This brings me back to my mom and my dad. They taught me much more than to have manners and think first about the other person or the larger community. They instilled in me the importance of asking questions, of not being bound by the false constraint that says being smart means you have to have all the answers, that it's a sign of strength to be fearless about saying out loud that you don't know and finding people to help you understand. They also taught me to build relationships and know those relationships will grow and change over time. They didn't want me to feel constrained by the initial interaction, especially in a professional relationship.

Several years ago, chance reconnected me with my favorite elementary school teacher. I was speaking at a conference for women entrepreneurs and executives, and Eileen was in the audience. Afterward, she came up to me and asked if I remembered her. There was no way I didn't (and I suspect she knew it). Eileen had been one of those magical teachers who truly believe in their students (all of them), who have high standards and know how to make us believe we could achieve them. She invited me to lunch and toward the end asked if I'd be open to hearing about her new project.

Fast-forward to today, and we are business partners working to bring to life her idea, now our idea. At first it was hard to call Eileen by her first name, but she led the way by honoring that we were now peers; we were not bound by the constraints of our former relationship of teacher and student.

I have to say here that my willingness to challenge constraints doesn't take away from recognizing that some constraints have to be respected (not the least of which are that there are only 24 hours in a day and that being a good citizen means wearing a mask to protect not just yourself but those around you). What's important is to see constraints clearly for what they are.

There is one constraint I know can't be changed, even though it's painful for me: It's the one that says no one bats 1,000%. There are some opportunities we get right and some we don't, and needing to figure out how to deal with both is a constraint there's no way to avoid. What does help me is loving the process, and knowing that my citizenship today comes from helping the communities I'm part of, as a member or a leader, liberate themselves from unnecessary or outdated constraints and grow. It fuels my perennial optimism for what's possible for all of us.

---

*A serial entrepreneur and a pioneer in the New York technology community, **Beth Polish** is the founder of The Critical Junctures Group, which helps companies and leaders turn constraints into opportunities for change and growth. She was founding COO/CFO of iVillage; President of Dreamlife, Inc., co-founded with Tony Robbins; CFO of Goldman Sachs Ventures; and Head of Corporate Innovation at Hearst Corporation. She has an MBA from Harvard and a BS in anthropology.*

https://www.linkedin.com/in/bethpolish/

Never Give Up!

By Darcy Verhun, *President at FYidoctors*

"I love those who can smile in trouble, who can gather strength from distress, and grow brave by reflection."
— Leonardo Da Vinci

Sometimes things don't turn out like we dreamed, and that's not a bad thing. I grew up in northern Alberta, Canada, with dreams of becoming a world-famous ski racer. Those were lofty aspirations for a kid living on the edge of the prairies where the largest ski hill ran down the banks of the North Saskatchewan River at Rabbit Hill – with a whopping 274-foot vertical drop.

One of my idols, "Jungle" Jim Hunter, had grown up in Saskatchewan, where the ski hills were even smaller and the prairies even flatter. He had gone on to win a Bronze Medal in the World Championships – so I knew it was possible. Just because everything about a situation makes it appear impossible doesn't mean you can't aspire to achieve your goal.

So, I poured my entire being into making my dream happen.

It was a long road. Finally, at age 23, while too old to make the Canadian ski team, I found myself getting closer to my dream. I secured my first-ever "first-seed" starting bib for an Alberta Cup Slalom race at Mount Norquay, Banff. Boy, was I ready. Being a first seed is super important because the course is still smooth and not rutted from all the racers having gone before. I was given bib number 5, and I thought to myself that I had finally arrived. A couple weeks before, I had placed fourth in a race, having to work from a later seed and a rutted ski hill, and I just knew I would stand on the top of the podium this weekend.

I spent the night before tuning my skis to perfection, got a good night's sleep, and by the morning I was ready to go. I got to the hill early, making sure everything was in place and I was ready to rip. The run next to the race pitch was called Rascal, also known as Area 13 on the map. I thought to myself that it would be a great place to warm up – 13 was my lucky number, after all.

I had been coached to do slow looping turns while warming up, feeling the entire ski, and finding my balance. All was going fine, but halfway down the test run something happened. Life threw me an unexpected curve ball.

While making a right-hand turn, I fell backward into the hill and somehow managed to hook the tail of my downhill ski under the uphill ski as I fell slowly backward. This locked my lower left leg in place while my body fell away from my lower leg. Something had to give – and it did. I did not know it at the time, but I managed to tear my ACL completely off my femur.

I lay there alone with a few silent tears of pain. Once I managed to get up, I tried to ski the pain off. Being a ski racer, fear was not something I allowed into my psyche. I told myself that I could not possibly be hurt. I wasn't long on patience, either.

I needed to get to the starting gate no matter what. I needed to race!

When something goes wrong or you find yourself against a new and seemingly impenetrable barrier, should you quit?

"I'll quit competing when my heart quits beating."
— Michael Jordan

Luckily, the race run was only accessible by a T-bar lift, so my leg did not have to hang in the air while on a chair lift. The race organizers had cut the trees down above the lift, creating an extension up the hill, so that the race could start higher. After taking my skis off to hike to the start, I discovered I could not actually lift my leg to climb up the hill to the starting gate. I stood there, four or five slalom gates from the start, in total dismay, watching my competitors fly by as they raced down the course.

My dream of a podium that weekend felt shattered. I had no choice but to call it a day, but I was determined I would be ready by the next day.

That was not meant to be. A trip to the emergency room that afternoon told me I would need surgery to repair my knee. That surgery to repair my ACL resulted in a leg infection that had me in the hospital for almost the entire summer, with the doctors barely managing to save my leg from amputation. Ultimately, they were able to save my leg, but I no longer had the physical capability to race at the highest levels. I can still rip around the mountain pretty well, thankfully, but 100+ KPH downhill races were completely a no-go.

Is it possible to turn a door that has closed to an unfulfilled dream, the ultimate constraint, into a new reality?

I used the newfound time lying there recovering to reinvent myself, to apply the skills I'd learned in pursuit of ski racing to something completely new. I was forced to learn the virtues of patience. While spending the next year in physiotherapy working on range of motion and strength, I decided to attend classes at university.

In school, I learned to love learning. I discovered many things I had never considered or was aware of, and I learned that I actually did not know as much as I thought I did about pretty much everything. Attending undergraduate and then graduate education created new possibilities for me – which in turn opened unseen doors and proved to totally change my life. Those lessons include:

Dealing with reality – I had to adapt and change in ways that did not align with my dreams at that time. I had to deal with the realities of the situation. No matter how I tried – my dream would not happen. Sometimes accepting and being open to the reality of the situation allows us to move on, which can be enough. And the things we have learned until then do provide a foundation to our path forward. They also provide linkages to the core attributes of what makes each of us special and able to carry on in the face of adversity.

Learning mindset – University taught me how to learn, which, in turn, has opened my eyes to things I had never imagined. I certainly could have figured this out without higher education, so I want to be clear that school is not the key point here. Day in and day out, I believe that if you aren't learning – you are most certainly dying. Like unprotected metal left outside, you are in fact rusting away. Being open to and investing in learning allows you to be able to adapt, grow, and achieve things you had previously thought impossible.

Being a ski racer at heart – I believe that the attributes of a racer include balance, work ethic, constant adaptability, fearlessness even when you are actually afraid, and always looking ahead anticipating what you can't even see yet on the other side of a knoll. While I will never achieve that dream, I am able to do my best to apply the attributes of a ski racer to my life. So, I'm feeling in a roundabout way that perhaps I am actually realizing my dreams, albeit on a different pitch.

Over the years since then, I have had many opportunities to apply and build on those learnings.

"The only thing we know about the future is that it is going to be different."
– Peter Drucker

In my current leadership role, I serve as president of a diversified healthcare company with 300 locations, a team of over 3,000 colleagues and 630 Optometrist Doctors. I see those lessons I discovered in my youth still apply. Things can and will happen that you don't expect and require you to adapt and create new opportunities. I could never have anticipated the impact and challenges that COVID-19 would place on us. Things came at us quickly during 2020, and because we did not know much about what would happen, we had to react and be in the moment.

The year before had been a best-ever milestone year for FYidoctors, and the start of 2020 provided every indication we would do even better. My team and I were wearing "first-seed" starting bibs. Enter another curve ball. As eye health care providers, we quickly recognized that what we saw happening was like no other crisis, and in order to successfully navigate this, we needed our leadership team to think and act differently. We knew we needed to come from a place of empathy, which was already the core of our DNA of "Enhancing Life." At the same time, we needed to ensure that the patient experience we delivered continued to be safe and trusted. Every action we took, and how we acted as leaders, aligned with these three pillars: flexibility, empathy, and delivering a safe and trusted patient experience.

Early in March 2020, while still not quite believing what was happening, we decided to band together an Emergency Response Team of forty-three people in various roles from coast to coast. We held virtual daily meetings first thing each morning. The agenda evolved each day as we worked to stay balanced, and working to anticipate and prepare for what was next, we remained tuned to the needs of our colleagues on the front line providing emergency eye care in our clinics. We did not fully know it at the time, but we were effectively taking steps in real-time to adapt to a barrier there was no getting around.

We empowered leaders in our clinics and home office departments to be able to provide their teams with greater flexibility on an individual needs' basis to ensure we never put our team or our patients at risk. As eye care professionals, following safe health protocols is paramount. During this pandemic, we went the extra mile and ramped up PPE and safety practices that go above and beyond regulated protocols to ensure our teams' and our patients' safety. We had to reinvent ourselves while leveraging our collective talent, prior experience, and knowledge.

Closing thoughts

The lessons that started the moment I crashed on that test run in my early twenties provided the foundation and confidence for me to be open to change, to adapt under pressure, to be able to look past the seemingly impossible, and practically apply a learning mindset in life and in business. It seems that life continues to throw up plenty of roadblocks to achieving my aspirations, and in every instance, being able to approach these with a never-quit mindset has resulted in new doors of possibility opening.

Sometimes constraints are insurmountable, and other times they are only a challenge to overcome. Both create new opportunities if you

search for them – anticipating what is yet unseen and beyond the knoll.
So, I will close with a few questions:

What impossible barriers have you faced in your life?

What unexpected opportunities did you realize and create as a result?

Can you uncover newfound ways to build on your experiences to create new dreams and shape your future to achieve them?

Darcy *remains a lifelong learner, working to embrace new challenges and continuing to build from life's lessons learned. Darcy is the President of FYidoctors, an organization focused on "Enhancing life." He has been recognized as a Fellow of the Chartered Professional Accountants of Canada and is a distinguished alumnus of MacEwan University. Darcy is an aspiring author and will always be a ski racer in life.*

https://www.linkedin.com/in/darcy-verhun/

Leadership Clarity
is Born
from Adversity

*"You are ready to aid in the shaping and application
of those wise constraints that make men free."*
– John MacArthur Maguire, *LL.B Harvard 1911*

T
he following insights into adversity teach us how leaders
address challenges, and are written from the lens of those
who have been in leadership roles or who currently coach
executives in the trenches. Discover how your individual
perspectives have a direct link to your ability as a leader to
move beyond the challenges that you or your team face. This
section will help you understand the internal views that may
hold you back, why courage is such a key leadership attribute,
and how displaying courage can help you unlock innovation
when faced with obstacles.

Discernment Can Break Constraints and Free Up Creativity for Productivity

By Richie Norton, *Award-Winning Author of the Power of Starting Something Stupid*

"A great deal of creativity is about pattern recognition, and what you need to discern patterns is tons of data. Your mind collects that data by taking note of random details and anomalies easily seen every day: quirks and changes that, eventually, add up to insights."
— Margaret Heffernan

I live on the warm North Shore of Oahu and had always wanted to visit New York City. When I finally got the chance, I braved the cold and visited Times Square, saw the Statue of Liberty, rode the subway, visited Ground Zero, and walked through Central Park.

One of my life's mini-dreams was achieved when I visited the Empire State Building. I was presented with two tourist experience options: the standard trip to the observation deck, where they filmed the famous scene from Sleepless in Seattle, or I could pay an additional $15 fee to go just a few flights higher.

Like most people I'd imagine, I thought, *Why would I pay more just to go a little higher?* But I figured since I'd already invested so much time, effort, and money to get all the way to New York in the first place, I might as well pay a few dollars more to go to the tippy top.

The view from the 102nd floor was amazing! While the 86th floor general observation deck had been PACKED with people squeezing through crowds to get a glimpse of the scene below, the small fee that landed me on the 102nd floor sifted out the competition and left plenty of room to enjoy the sights. I could effortlessly see the Brooklyn Bridge, the Statue of Liberty, and a million amazing buildings in the distance. It was worth every penny of my small investment.

As I rode the old-fashioned elevator back down from the 102nd floor, a recorded voice came over the speaker and said, "You are now a member of the Elite 102 Club!" I didn't even know there was a club, and now I was a part of it! In that moment, I learned a significant life lesson.

There's room at the top because so few are willing to pay the extra price to get there.

The constraint of the extra price, as I call it, created an additional opportunity at the top. Every constraint in business and life is a "price to pay" to get to where you want to go.

It's a small price to pay, but investing a little extra effort into the life you choose will move you from average — where all the competition is — to the top.

WHAT DO YOU SEE FIRST?

If you saw the rabbit first, did you look for and find the duck? If you saw the duck first, did you look for and find the rabbit?

This illustration is a poignant example that constraints are largely in our mind. There are many ways to achieve a goal, and constraints pressure us to discover new ways to accomplish those goals. Once you see another way, you can't unsee it — like seeing both animals in this drawing.

The practice of becoming aware of constraints, overcoming them, and achieving your aim through constraints (or something better) begins with having a significant challenge at hand. Please consider a current challenge and look for the "rabbit" or "duck" that you're not seeing as you read this essay. I promise that as you learn to see solutions that may already be present, you'll also become more creative, more data-driven (as you gather intel), and more trustworthy (and trusting) as you make wise decisions in uncertain situations.

Once you understand the value of constraints, your life will suddenly be free. With freedom, you'll be better abled to provide joy to those you serve with intentional attention.

Discernment will be the Key Competency of this Decade

Charles Dickens may have captured the essence of 2010-2020 best in *A Tale of Two Cities* when he said, "It was the age of wisdom, it was the age of foolishness."

> *"It was the best of times, it was the worst of times, it was the age of wisdom, it was the age of foolishness, it was the epoch of belief, it was the epoch of incredulity, it was the season of Light, it was the season of Darkness, it was the spring of hope, it was the winter of despair, we had everything before us, we had nothing before us, we were all going direct to Heaven, we were all going direct the other way..."*

> *— Charles Dickens, A Tale of Two Cities*

Certainly, the decade of 2010 was an age of wisdom and foolishness, an age of massive technological change and business, an age of information and misinformation, an age of global calamities, and local heroisms in the age of social wellness and social illness.

...and it's not slowing down.

What have we learned?

How have constraints helped us achieve our aims despite unconventional challenges? Where do we go from here?

The pace of change in society, business, and our personal lives is accelerating in unprecedented ways. Our leaders are largely unprepared to handle challenges that we can't foresee at such high speeds. We are forging into unknown territory. This "brave new world" requires a different level of thinking for coaches, leaders, and executives to shape the environments in which we desire to live and thrive.

So what do we do?

Discernment Leadership & Discernment Entrepreneurship

Discernment is a learnable skill.

Discernment is the key to greater acts of character and competence under high constraints.

Discernment offsets constraints to achieve goals when we lack creativity, data, and trust.

Discernment gives us the ability to make wise decisions when we are in hostile, complicated, or unusual environments.

This essay explores how we can identify, overcome, stretch, and even work outside constraints using the power of discernment. Namely, we'll discuss what I call the three converging principles of discernment: 1) creativity, 2) data, and 3) trust to counteract constraints and make wise decisions. The time has come for leaders to consciously, thoughtfully, and intentionally practice discernment.

I predict:

Discernment will become the number one leadership competency of the decade — the age of misinformation.

Leaders, entrepreneurs, and individuals who learn to discern will have the unique and rare advantage to help more people, add more value, and create better experiences for those they care for, love, and serve.

Those who cannot discern will be fooled by misdirection and misdirection-data, and lose their productive creativity to increasing opportunity cost (and won't know until it's too late).

The ability and skill to prepare and create what is yet to come is discernment.

THE THREE CONVERGING PRINCIPLES OF DISCERNMENT TO OFFSET CONSTRAINTS DERIVED FROM DATA

1. Creativity as the Key Leadership Competency

In 2010, creativity becomes the number one competency for leaders.

NY — 18 May 2010: According to a major new IBM (NYSE: IBM) survey of more than 1,500 Chief Executive Officers from 60 countries and 33 industries worldwide, chief executives believe that "more than rigor, management discipline, integrity, or even vision — successfully navigating an increasingly complex world will require creativity."

2. Data Access as the Key Leadership Competency

By the end of the decade, in stark contrast to creativity, data access has become the key.

"In our latest Global C-suite Study, we asked more than 13,000 C-suite executives what it takes to lead in a world brimming with bytes.... The CEOs who help run these organizations aren't daunted by data; on the contrary, they're using it to make smarter business decisions, build stronger ecosystems, and experiment with new business models."

3. Trust as the Key Leadership Competency

In fact, in 2021, IBM's latest research took it a step further with this statement: "Our latest study draws on input from 13,484 respondents across 6 C-suite roles, 20 industries, and 98 countries.... We learned that data-driven leadership is determined by the levels of trust an organization can create — among its customers, the people inside the enterprise, and the partners across its ecosystem."

DISCERNMENT IS THE KEY LEADERSHIP COMPETENCY OF THIS DECADE

The pendulum of the top leadership skill over a decade swung from the creative polar to the data access and then centered itself in the middle on trust. Good news: Creativity, data, and trust are drivers of success. And yet... The world has entered an age of misinformation at such a global, instant scale that it is hard to discern what is truth and what isn't.

Creative problem solving with bad data doesn't solve problems — it creates more.

On the other hand, we may have never had more access to accurate information. Like the image of the duck-rabbit above, two truths (or more) can exist simultaneously. Two people could observe the image, and one could argue that the illustrator drew a duck and then stop the argument there. Would that be true? Yes. But is there a rabbit? Yes. The discerning truth is that the drawing is both! The discerning truth sees asynchronous perspectives. Your job as a discerning leader is to seek, find, and share the discerning truth.

HOW TO USE DISCERNMENT TO OFFSET CONSTRAINTS AND FREE UP CREATIVITY FOR HIGH PRODUCTIVITY

When faced with a constraint, do these four activities:

- **Get creative** – What would you do if that constraint didn't exist? Is there another way to do that? Think of 10 different ways you could achieve the same goal.

- **Gather data** – What are you unaware of? What are you not seeing? Why didn't you see it before? Are others seeing what you're seeing? Who cares about this issue/project/goal? Why do you care, and what is the ideal outcome you and your stakeholders would want if the constraint didn't exist? Create a shared vision of the new perspectives with the stakeholders.

- **Trust others** – Avoid asking how to achieve the objective. Ask who can help you make the objective happen. Find trustworthy people to help you execute on a shared mission. Don't go it alone.

- **Leverage discernment** – Ask yourself how you can a) achieve the goal, b) without the negative thing you're worried about happening, c) within your desired timeline. After doing steps 1-3, you may come up short and not have the creative, data, or trustworthy resources. Tap into discernment by creating an environment for what is not "yet" but what you want to have happen. Remember: The ability and skill to prepare and create what is yet to come is discernment.

To find simple, actionable solutions, we need discerning leaders to strike at the heart of things and see constraints as a way to pay the price to free up our creativity for greater productivity.

In closing, I want to share an experience when my lack of discernment opened up opportunities for its use. One morning at the beach, I went to start my car, only to realize the gas tank was empty. The fact I had driven all day without noticing the amount of gas in the tank showed my lack of discernment. I headed down the street to the nearest gas station and asked the attendant if he had a gas can I could borrow. Before he could answer, the stranger in line behind me spoke up and said that he had a full gas can in his van that I could use.

I needed help, and a stranger had offered a gift. For a split second, I wanted to say no. But, I reminded myself of the power of receiving and told myself to give it a go.

I thanked the stranger over and over while apologizing profusely for the inconvenience. To add to my already heightened feelings of awkwardness, it turned out that he was originally headed in the opposite direction. However, the stranger was unaffected by this revelation and still cheerfully insisted on driving me back to my car.

When I climbed into his van and looked around, two things were immediately evident. First, the man was a struggling landscaper, and second, he loved to fish. Rusty landscaping equipment, dozens of old fishing poles, and the strong aroma of dead fish filled the back of the van. He told me that he and his coworker had just finished fishing and were now headed to a job. When I asked about his work, he explained how he'd recently lost a lot of income but was optimistic. "I'll never be rich," he said, with bright, happy eyes, "but it gets me by."

He took me to my car, and I humbly put this stranger's gas into my tank. But my car was parked at a very steep angle, so even the amount of gas from the full gas can wasn't enough. The car still wouldn't start. I felt horrible. I was so embarrassed to be further inconveniencing this nice stranger.

Again, he was unaffected; in fact, he was genuinely happy to help. On our way back to the gas station, I saw that his "empty" light was on. I was surprised he hadn't run out of gas trying to help me! It suddenly occurred to me: This stranger wasn't at the gas station to fill up his van — he didn't have enough money to do that — he was there to fill up the gas can for his landscaping equipment... the very gas can he had so generously offered to me.

As I finished filling the small gas can, I then turned to the stranger and I offered him a gift.

"I want to put some gas in your van," I said.

He shook his head no. "Karma," he smiled. "It always comes back to help me. That's how I've gotten by all these years." He continued adamantly, "I didn't help you to profit."

I understood his feelings, but believing that karmic law was surely reciprocating his kindness right here and now, I insisted and filled up his van. This stranger's gift to me had been returned to him tenfold — unexpectedly and immediately.

What constraints in your life (empty gas tank, for example) can turn into new opportunities and freedoms, and bless others through discernment?

Richie Norton is the award-winning author of "The Power of Starting Something Stupid" (in 10+ languages). He is the founder of Global Consulting Circle, coaching founders on creating / scaling final cause business models. He is the Co-Founder of PROUDUCT — helping entrepreneurs innovate from idea to market through full-service product-to-fulfillment. Richie is featured in Forbes, Businessweek, Entrepreneur, HuffPo, Inc., etc., and is an international speaker, entrepreneur, and podcaster. Richie is happily married, has four boys, and lives on the North Shore of Oahu, Hawaii.

https://richienorton.com/

Limitation is Definition

By Scott Osman, *CEO at 100 Coaches*

"The enemy of art is the absence of limitation."
— Orson Welles

love science museums. When my children were young, we used to go to the Montshire Museum of Science in Vermont and spend hours with all of the exhibitions and experiments that they offered. One particularly mesmerizing exhibit was the water flow with obstacles table. It enabled you to see the flow of water, and then by placing obstacles in the path, you could change the direction of the flow, the speed, and even where sand developed mounds or valleys. In this water-flow table, I see the metaphor for the value of limitations and the importance of using them wisely.

The obstacles we place in the flow of the water are what we use to define the water flow. They are not constraints; they are definitions. Some limitations are not under our control, so we need to accept them as unmovable definers; others are under our control, and we can use them to create the definition we desire.

Whether we are thinking as a leader about our team or as an individual about ourselves, we use our limitations to define ourselves.

For 12 months, we meditated on the limitations we have as individuals, as leaders, as a society, and as an ecosystem. Among the pandemic's many teachings, one is to consider how we are not really in as much control as we thought. COVID-19 gave us immediate feedback on the price of ignoring the problem, avoiding taking action, and the value of adapting quickly. Some businesses saw the obstacle and adjusted.

My friend Marc Sternberg of Brand Innovators, a live conference business, was two weeks away from his SXSW event, one of his four pillars of the year, when the event was canceled. A true entrepreneur, he did not waste any time worrying about why the problem happened; he focused all of his energy on defining his business by the new limitations. He understood that the real asset he had created was not events, it was community, and right now, the community was a premium product. Without much experience in virtual events, he took his entire three venues' four-day lineup online. His members showed up, his sponsors supported him, and his business soared. He is now in the virtual community business and is exceeding his previous year's numbers.

Sometimes the limitations are not external; they are our imagination. A leader's role is to set a vision, build the team to execute that vision, and then support and hold the members accountable to do their work. Successful leaders understand how to recognize the market's limitations and set the limitations to keep their company focused. My good friend Martin Lindstrom is a master at helping CEOs rethink their vision, reset their brand, and reshape their culture. The story of Lowe's Supermarket is a story of imagining the possible and making the changes necessary to create and execute a new vision for an old business.

When Martin was brought in to help the company, a frequent customer reply to the question "Why do you shop at Lowe's?" was "Because there is no other place to shop." Lowe's was not a lousy supermarket; it was an ordinary one. The vision was of a place to put products on shelves, and customers would come and take the products off shelves. It was the world many people expect of a supermarket, devoid of creativity and delight. And that was the expectation of the employees, and it was what they delivered.

With the CEO's bravery and ambition, and Martin's creativity and lots of research, they set about rethinking the idea of a supermarket and what could make it a place that people wanted to go to rather than had to go to. They accepted the limitations of a supermarket as a place you purchase a product, and added a new limitation that it could not be seen as a waste of time. They knew that consumers were time-starved, and they needed to find a way to make the experience something the customer would look forward to. They conceived a story that was an entertainment experience, hired employees who liked to perform, and found ways to make every interaction fun. The result was delighted employees, enthusiastic customers, and explosive growth.

Leadership and life are defined by the obstacles we face and the opportunities we make of them. The truth is, a limitation is simply a barrier. It forces us to change course, think differently, overcome, go around, back down. It pushes us out of our comfort zone to be creative. It tests us, advances us, stretches us, begs us to be better.

Our future is going to be defined by limitations and how we are defined by them. We have had an unprecedented period of growth and lack of adversity over the past 75 years (you can pick your own period). With the end of WWII, we have been free from the massive carnage of global wars. The advent and application of science set us free from many diseases, thanks to vaccines and treatments. Growth in the economy has allowed for a general but inequitable increase in the quality of life. We have enjoyed a carefree relationship with our environment.

The year of living pandemically was a test of how we respond to limitations. A fundamental limitation was that we can no longer think that we can solve problems alone. There is no way to stay safe during a pandemic by yourself. Each one of us needed to take individual responsibility, and we needed to rely on others. If we were lucky enough to work from home, we required frontline workers willing to pick up and deliver our groceries, truck drivers to deliver packages, nurses and doctors to tend to those who got sick — the list is long. If we masked when we went outside, we relied on others to do the same.

The other side of the limitations was the economic devastation in specific industries and in the lives of so many people who couldn't work. The trillions of dollars we are investing in supporting the economy and individuals who bear the brunt are a measure of the scale we face.

As the CEO of 100 Coaches, I learn from some of the best leaders, leading thinkers, and leadership coaches in the world. The same lessons we know about leadership also apply to our lives. We cannot do everything. We have limitations, and how we address them will define us. And limitations will come in all forms – money, skills, access, health, networks, and the most significant limitation of all, time. They will define us.

The most powerful way I have observed that we can overcome limitations is by working together. Finding a community that you support and supports you creates greater capacity. Finding a team that has complementary skills creates leverage. Learning from others and building on their knowledge amplifies our abilities. The more significant and more complex the problem, organization, or ambition, the more the need to be supported by teams of teams who can create efficient scale solutions. Limitations define us.

Teams can defy limitations.

Most of the time, we only think about our part of the water table, thinking that we are in control. We observe how the currents flow, move some stones here or there, and change the direction to suit our needs. Other times, we make more significant moves, erecting structures seemingly as massive as the Hoover Dam to create new entities, grow new value, and bring new ideas to life. Within our worlds, we can seem powerful as we shift the flows. Other times, stones are being placed, creating limitations, and forcing us to adapt to the changing currents.

The pandemic is a limitation wake-up call. The new investments being made in the economy, the faster adoption of working from home, and the realization that big problems cannot be addressed by individuals must be addressed by society changing the flow in dramatic ways. It a call to extreme creativity and imagination to recognize that the world has changed. The pandemic challenges present an opportunity to see life through a new lens, to use the new limitations to redefine ourselves and our society. The pandemic reminds us of our humanity and our limitations, and it exposes the value of working together. That's a good thing. Now it's time to put that to use.

Scott Osman *leads Marshall Goldsmith's 100 Coaches organization, a curated community of the world's top leaders, leadership coaches, and leadership thinkers. Previously global director of Purpose Branding at Landor Associates, Scott has decades of experience in leading brand and innovation strategy to deliver meaningful and measurable leadership and culture change. With Marshall, he is currently developing the Marshall Goldsmith Leadership Development online curriculum and is co-authoring a new book, Leadership is a Team Sport.*

scott@100coaches.com

Leadership Lessons from Coaching During the Pandemic

By David Slocum, Ph.D., *Academic Director and Program Adviser at RARE by Google* and Doug Guthrie, *Professor at the Thunderbird School of Global Management*

"Bad companies are destroyed by crisis, Good companies survive them, Great companies are improved by them."
— Andy Grove (1994)

Leadership is Practice, Leadership is Social, Leadership is Everyday

I n the last few decades, society has come to worship the charismatic leader – strong in crisis, magnetic in personality, and passionate of vision. Yet, after years of the born-to-lead culture, today's public space is sorely lacking individuals who are capable of mastering their organizations, inspiring change, and, most important, leading through a crisis. This is especially true today, as we ride the disorienting waves of fear and indecision associated with the coronavirus pandemic, widespread geopolitical disaffection, and political unrest in multiple countries across the world. This moment, with its complexity and fragmentation, demands a new type of leader and an improved approach to leadership development.

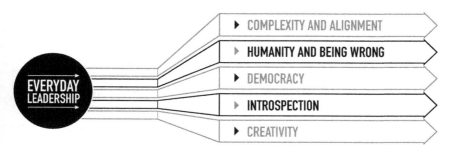

Our approach to teaching and coaching rising leaders focuses on action-oriented coaching and an approach we call everyday leadership. And in a number of ways, the pandemic has allowed us – indeed forced us – to think about teaching and coaching these concepts over great distances and new media. When our students and clients ask us today, "When do you think things are going to return to normal?" our answer is often, "Maybe never. Assume never and focus on how to connect with your team and the people around you in new ways and over new media. Think about how to take the constraints of the pandemic and learn new lessons, models, and methods of leadership."

Everyday leaders, quite simply, are forged in the day-to-day work of teams, organizations, and wider systems; that only by mastering organizational and human complexity can leaders align strategy with organizational dynamics; and that leaders must know themselves and be alert to their failings and graces, in order to better serve the organization. The anchors of our framework are organized around five key themes: complexity and alignment, humility and being wrong, democracy, introspection, and creativity. The question becomes:

"How do we teach and otherwise enable these skills and this approach to leadership over great distance and with virtual teams?"

Everyday Leadership's main components

Complexity and alignment – Leaders must embrace complexity for the opportunities it holds, both the complexity of the team, organization, or system, and of the human dynamics shaping and animating it.

Only by deeply engaging these intricate patterns, relationships, and interdependencies can leaders align organizational or other collective forms and functions, and craft strategies that create new and unexpected avenues for shared growth and innovation.

Humility and being wrong – Leaders must have an innate understanding of who they are and be able to define their strengths and weaknesses. While some debate whether acknowledging weakness and apologizing for errors undermines leaders, we contend that by admitting mistakes, acknowledging blind spots, and embracing errors and failures, leaders can gain credibility and trust within the organization. Humility is a powerful tool for personal and institutional growth.

Democracy – Individuals at every level of the organization are capable of leadership, and leadership is fundamentally social. In fact, the success of the organization depends on each individual being empowered to lead, because leaders are not born; they mature through continuing relationships in the workplace and in civic life.

Introspection – Everyday leaders do not lead by intuition or charisma alone, but instead by having the patience to think analytically and creatively about how the parts of their organizations fit together as a whole. They think about, feel, and otherwise engage deeply their roles in their teams or organizations and how best to lead – or to evolve as leaders – based on their profound understanding of themselves and their institutional cultures.

Creativity – The infinite complexity of the organization and the individuals who make up its workforce should be celebrated. Good leaders understand that complexity adds depth, and they embrace it. When leaders follow the typical mindset of strategy and economics, they gravitate toward what is common, comfortable, and known. By embracing creativity, leaders can find endless opportunities to discover something new. The real world is much more exciting and interesting, and it requires creativity in its leaders to respond to the unpredictable moment.

Some may even wonder about the description of our approach: Everyday Leadership. The dictionary definition of "everyday" is simple: "an adjective that means commonplace, ordinary, or normal." Describing our leaders as common or ordinary doesn't diminish our view of the everyday leader. In fact, we believe it elevates the notion, becoming a way of being marked by profound simplicity in the face of complexity, and ensuring equity and agency for everyday leaders in every position in an organization.

Finally, this kind of leadership is built and sustained through everyday action because it insists on the full participation of everyone. Our leadership goal isn't the creation of effective leaders alone; it is the creation of successful teams, organizations, and systems that are guided by far-sighted, humble, and creative leaders.

Coaching Everyday Leadership Through the Pandemic and Beyond

We have both had the great privilege of being executive coaches and executive education educators for more than a decade. Our recurring priorities with clients include helping them think strategically and analytically about their organizations, grounding decisions and actions in their beliefs and values, committing to their and others' growth across different areas of their lives, and supporting choices and habit changes they know they should make but have great difficulty following through on. Our clients are senior leaders and business owners in industries ranging from big tech, marketing, and media to business intelligence and strategic consulting working in Europe, North America, and China. While the Coronavirus crisis has impacted each differently, we've observed several commonalities in the challenges and opportunities that many have been facing for more than a year.

Now, as leaders in much of Europe, North America, and China look to emerge from the worst of the Coronavirus crisis and begin the slow process of defining their next normal, we've continued to reflect on the coaching we've done since the pandemic overtook so many lives in early March of 2020. What defined many of our interactions with leaders at that time has continued to be important for them as the pandemic continues. Perhaps the most noticeable change has been their having to cope with the challenges of a persisting crisis: of sustaining high levels of energy, sleeping regularly, providing ongoing care and support for themselves and others, and avoiding being overwhelmed by continuing stress and uncertainty and the risk of burnout.

Here are some of the imperatives and priorities for leaders that we have learned about regarding the social aspects of Everyday Leadership through teaching and coaching during the pandemic:

Start from where you are. Determine how best to support all your people. Embrace the Stockdale Paradox: Never confuse your confidence and resolve that you'll prevail long term with the discipline to confront honestly the facts and uncertainty of the current reality.

Acknowledge and adapt your life boundaries being blurred by the crisis – at work, at home, with family, with friends, for yourself, in digital spaces. Don't double-down on what got you here; be open to making hard decisions and unexpected changes, and doing the hard, everyday work of learning (and unlearning) with others.

Communicate clearly, transparently, consistently, and with care – but don't overwhelm already stressed colleagues by over-communicating. Also, remember: Individuals have different communication, coaching, and feedback needs, so personalize whenever possible. For all, make sure you do what you say.

Focus on the human, practical, and concrete in your leadership decisions and actions. Execute your key priorities every day while keeping an eye on more-distant time horizons. More than ever, model your values, vulnerability, integrity, and what you want to see from others and in team or organizational interactions.

Match the internal pace of teams or organizations with external conditions (as Stanley McChrystal puts it), especially by adapting to new and evolving urgencies, the accelerated cadence of business, and the demands on you (and your teams) to sustain high levels of energy, emotion, and performance over time.

Be intentional about caring for others and caring for yourself. Sleep. Guard against information or emotional overload. Recognize that fears, anxieties, and uncertainties are both impacting people's work perform-ance and the rest of their lives and calling on all of us to lead more creatively, optimistically, supportively, and empathetically.

Put in the time and energy to answer, honestly, the essential question, "What do you really want? At work, in relationships, in life, for the world?" Then determine, "How will you achieve that?" In crises, espe-cially, also ask: "What do you really need? Physically, emotionally, psychologically, economically?"

Acknowledge you're frequently more driven to avoid losing what you have than to pursue what you want. **Loss aversion is real:** We prefer familiar unhappiness to unfamiliar happiness. Fear of working with less status or money, of eating or sleeping alone, of displaying weaknesses or vulnerability can easily trump a desire for constructive change. Be courageous and follow your North Star.

Do everything you can, respectfully, to understand and respond to what others want and need, what they fear, and how you can support the change(s) they seek in their lives. As a leader, colleague, confi-dante, loved one, or friend, tell them and show them you care. Often. Help them become (what they strive for, not just what you see, as) their best selves.

Expand and diversify the circles of friends, confidantes, and advisers who regularly surround and support you. Don't always (over-)rely on the same few or one. Assess your support systems – confront what they say about you, and recast them to help yourself learn and grow. Remember, as David Burkus recently argued: You're the average of all the people who surround you.

Know and act on your core principles and values. These are your most crucial guides to leading (and living) during crises and amidst uncer-tainty that defy conventional analysis or forecasting. Identify your values and beliefs, clarify how they orient you in given situations, and build your decisions, communications, and actions around them.

Determine how important this moment is for you, those you love or lead, your career or company, and the rest of your life. For some, it's a time for radical reinvention. For others, it's more about reinforcing current relationships or initiatives. For all, crises accelerate where you've been heading. Take time to understand what this crisis means for yourself and act accordingly (overcoming, as needed).

"The Pandemic is a Portal"

Early during the initial wave of the pandemic, on April 3, 2020, author Arundhati Roy published a short essay in the *Financial Times* entitled *"The Pandemic is a Portal."* Citing past epidemics, she emphasized the opportunity that the current Coronavirus crisis offered for positive social, economic, and, finally, human change. Roy concludes her piece with the following words of choice and possibility:

> *"Historically, pandemics have forced humans to break with the past and imagine their world anew. This one is no different. It is a portal, a gateway between one world and the next. We can choose to walk through it, dragging the carcasses of our prejudice and hatred, our avarice, our data banks and dead ideas, our dead rivers and smoky skies behind us. Or we can walk through lightly, with little luggage, ready to imagine another world. And ready to fight for it."*

The pandemic means something different to every leader, and each needs to determine how they'll manage and process it – as an opportunity to reimagine and remake their worlds or to stay largely on and tweak whatever course they've been on. Roy pushes hard on the opportunity offered by the crisis for substantive change, particularly social change. Her call to action is not only for leaders to reorganize their teams or businesses but to recast their thinking and relearn how to be more generous, inclusive, and humane. Drawing on Roy's article, we have recognized in our coaching how leaders do well to answer the following questions for themselves:

> *What's the most important leadership lesson of my experience of the pandemic?*

> *What's been most surprising about my experience of the pandemic? Why?*

What from my pre-pandemic life have I decided to give up or to leave behind?

What have I decided to (more fully) embrace or to take with us?

What change(s) do I hope for, and commit to supporting, on the other side?

What's the Bottom Line?

For better or worse, the pandemic has likely changed the ways in which leaders think about teams, organizations, and work in the world today. And that means a change for leadership. There will be changes in several key areas for leaders and how coaching may support them. Some of those will include:

The challenge of orientation and focus (or re-focus) on ourselves, others, and our responsibilities as leaders and citizens, to address both immediate and longer-term needs, amidst great uncertainty. For some who are used to succeeding in pressurized day-to-day routines, the pledge for the other side of the portal is to balance that everyday priority with more future thinking. That highlights the issue of (re-)defining boundaries and (re-)framing priorities for ourselves and others.

Unexpected perspectives on individual leadership and individual lives, and the realization that many are settling for a comfortable status quo (which they're fearful of losing). Most leaders want to be more courageous, and at work and elsewhere in their lives, make changes to develop their best selves. Many want to do more substantial and transformative work in the world, such as fighting for community, social, or political transformation.

Human/social dimensions of the crisis are paramount for leaders in all the roles that individuals play with family and friends, but also as community members and global citizens. Practically, this translates into caring more for self and others, avoiding being overwhelmed by circumstances, communicating openly and empathetically, demonstrating gratitude and loyalty, and committing to social or economic causes beyond oneself.

It is our hope that these ideas about leadership, teaching, and coaching in the shadow of this pandemic can help us understand a new model for coaching and leadership development. It is indeed an emergent new normal, the other side of a portal, and we look forward to future conversations over these issues that will guide and shape both leaders' growth and learning and the teaching and coaching practices that co-evolve with them.[2]

David Slocum, Ph.D., is Academic Director and Program Adviser at RARE by Google. David is also a Visiting Professor and Member of the Academic Advisory Board at the Berlin School of Creative Leadership (Steinbeis University, Germany), where he previously served as Faculty Director. David has nearly twenty years of global experience designing and facilitating training programs, and is a certified executive coach, with a focus on leadership, learning, and development, diversity and inclusion, and business creativity.

Doug Guthrie is Professor of Global Leadership and Director of China Initiatives at the Thunderbird School of Global Management. Previously, Guthrie was a Senior Director at Apple (2014-19), where he led Apple University efforts on leadership and organizational development in China; Dean of the George Washington School of Business (2010-13; Professor of Management and Director of custom Executive Education and Professor of Sociology (1997-2010); and the Founding Director of the University's Office of Global Education.

https://www.linkedin.com/in/dougguthrie/

---

[2] This essay combines two earlier articles published by David Slocum and Doug Guthrie at https://ongloballeadership.com. This current version combines insights from our work on coaching and everyday leadership.

Easier Said Than Done

By Bill Flynn, *Business Growth Coach* | *International Speaker* | *Entrepreneur* | *Author*

"Our acts of voluntary attending, as brief and fitful as they are, are nevertheless momentous and critical, determining us, as they do, to higher or lower destinies."
— William James

Startups and scaleups are full of constraints – money, resources, technology, people, time, experience, customers.
I have worked with and for many of each type. I sold what was futuristic speech recognition technology at Dragon Systems (now Nuance) back in 1991, then Open Market, the so-called Netscape of the East, where I met some of the smartest and most driven folks I have ever worked with. I have been through two IPOS and seven acquisitions, and helped dozens of businesses scale from humble beginnings – some to over $100M.

I have learned much from this three-decade journey. Here are three principles that have shaped my thinking:

1. Getting "through the knothole" at a startup is exceptionally difficult

Most do not have the stomach for it. Realizing that your original idea is unlikely to survive first contact with customers is a rare and humbling experience for founders – many remain unenlightened by the experience. After all, approximately three out of four of us think we are above average. The founder ratio must be close to 100%.

Here is how it usually goes.

You have a great idea (after all, everyone tells you it's great), and you spend a lot of time and money creating something wonderful. Then you start asking strangers to pay for it or spend their precious time using it and reality sets in (or does it?). Tip: When you hear yourself or others say "They just don't get it" following a few tough sales calls (let's go with 3), think about changing "they" to "I" and find out what you are missing fast before you run out of money!

Most founders fall in love with their idea instead of falling in love with the problem and the customer. They rarely realize that successful businesses fill an unmet need where enough customers will pay enough money for the business to drive a healthy profit and enough cash to fuel growth.

Easier said than done. You must constantly remind yourself and your team that no one cares what you do or make. They care about what it does for them. That is, the key struggle they are grappling with, the progress they are trying to make, the job(s) they are trying to get done.

2. Once through the knothole, there is no rest for the weary

Congratulations! You have now made it harder on yourself as your success has caught the attention of the market. Rivals will begin to sprout up. Many want some or all of what you have. Also, your investors are looking to see if you and your team can run a real business (ask me about the secret memo).

Celebrate. Take the weekend off. Get back to work on Monday. Stay focused. Keep innovating, because these days, it is a lot easier for competitors to quickly copy what you worked so hard and so long on to create. Even worse, they have the easier job of only having to figure out how to do it better, faster, and/or cheaper. (Also, where did all these team members come from anyway?!?)

Easier said than done. Many folks get sucked into the day-to-day running of the current business and lose sight of and touch with... you guessed it... customers and team members.

3. Well past the knothole. Focused on scaling (done totally differently from above)

Most of the things done and the decisions made happened organically or by accident, often driven by survival. Now you have to revisit every important decision, ensuring each is being done deliberately with a common purpose and direction. You will do well to have no sacred cows, as focusing on the few things that truly matter to your team and customers is your best bet.

Having studied business success for over thirty years, I have found that there are three main areas to focus on to scale a healthy and thriving business:

1. Teams (and teams of teams), for performance is a team sport.

2. Building a coherent leadership operating system focused on executing a differentiating strategy.

3. Using cash as your primary financial growth metric.

The most successful leaders do these things extremely well.

When this stage is reached, Founders/CEOs who do not realize that their "product" changed from being the product(s) they sell to being the business itself do so at their peril.

You now have to lead. That means letting go of almost everything you used to do and working on the business instead of in the business. You coach instead of do. You paint a vivid picture of the future for your team, create the roadmap with and for them, and show them how they contribute to the journey. Create a culture of learning, openness, and innovation.

You have to scale but not run out of money. Growth sucks cash ahead of itself.

When you are expendable to the operational side of the business, those three critical decisions of team, system, and cash are well in hand. You have now fired yourself from the day-to-day, for the most part, and can concentrate the majority of your time and effort on predicting the future of the business.

Easier said than done. CEOs are easily seduced by the siren song of the day-to-day operations – decisions they have become comfortable with. Some become insulated, some complacent. As growth happens, we begin to lose touch with our most important stakeholders – team members and customers (there they are again).

If you have gotten this far, it is time to focus on leading. Be courageous. I believe that courage is the only attribute that ALL leaders have in common.

Courage combined with a compelling and clear vision is critical to an enduring and valuable company.

Courage to defend and promote that unique and compelling vision.

Courage to be vulnerable.

Courage to create an autonomous environment.

Courage to trust that autonomy.

Courage to invest in mistakes as learning toward future growth.

Courage to be patient.

Courage to stop doing what gives you comfort and confidence.

Courage to go out on a limb to create the future.

Courage to surround yourself with a team that pushes and challenges you while simultaneously helping you see and craft that future.

You can be humble (Mulally) or not (Gates). You can be charismatic

(Kelleher) or not (Buffett). You can have empathy (Ardern) or not (Bezos). You can have integrity (Mulcahy) or not (Jobs). You can be honest (Aurelius) or not (LBJ). You can be loving (Chapman) or not (Musk).

The one thing all of these different people have in common is COURAGE in one form or another. We can argue how great, or not, each of these leaders is/was, but it is hard to deny each has/had courage.

If you have gotten this far, you should know that you are in rare company. Most businesses fail and many of the survivors are struggling – few thrive.

If you have gotten to five years where half of your peers have failed or fifteen where a mere twenty-five percent are still standing, you are in elite company. You truly are exceptional. You have created jobs, built phenomenal teams, and helped the economy to grow among myriad other contributions in which you have been instrumental. Truly a wonderful accomplishment. On behalf of millions of others, I thank you. Keep up the great work!

If you have not yet made it past these difficult hurdles, there are plenty of folks out there who can and want to help. Reach out, read a book (maybe mine!), try some stuff, fail and try again, and ask good questions. If you truly are out to solve a problem that is meaningful to enough people and you lead well, it will likely happen. But don't run out of cash!

Easier said than done. Remember that to lead a great company, the most important thing you need to do is to create the atmospheric conditions for success and then get out of the way.

Be exceptional!

---

*As a coach, in addition to being connected with MG 100, Women's Business Collaborative, MassMEP, Small Giants, and EforAll, **Bill** has earned certifications from ScalingUp, Gravitas Impact, Metronome United, Predictive Index, and The Neuroleadership Institute. Bill also published a bestselling book, "Further, Faster," in 2020.*

www.catalystgrowthadvisors.com

Personal High-Performance Practices Enhance Your Professional Success

By Bill Carrier, *President at Carrier Leadership Coaching Inc.*

"Energy, not time, is the fundamental currency of high performance."
— Jim Loehr

This is one of the comments I always make at the beginning of a new executive coaching engagement. As I said this to the CEO in front of me, he looked at me over his cup of coffee, as almost always occurs at first, and responded with a look that mixed skepticism and an almost forlorn hope.

I've had this short conversation many, many times. And, after working together for a few months, my clients and I have always been able to return to the subject with life-changing positive outcomes. They'd overcome the hidden habits and outdated social norms that drove them to focus on action instead of impact. They'd found the simple secret to enduring, sustainable, enjoyable high-performance.

This story is about a time I needed that help myself in order to keep helping others.

On Thursday of the week in March 2020 that the pandemic first became a big concern in the U.S., my wife and I were quarreling about something we normally didn't even notice. In general, we found ourselves a bit edgy and distracted. The uncomfortable state had crept up on us in between the long hours of stress and support for others because we'd both spent the early part of the week talking with clients and friends, calming some, informing others. Some of my CEO clients were asking for help to just figure out how to even begin thinking about their response to the pandemic.

That Thursday, Julie and I paused our argument, not because we ran out of fuel, but because it finally dawned on us that we were arguing because we were too tired—not for any substantive reason. We realized that we were drained by the week and it was only Thursday—and, much worse, we were already feeling the stress effects of what it is like to be living through a pandemic—and this was likely just the beginning.

I knew this was an important moment for us—and for our clients. We needed to immediately pivot into taking much better care of ourselves, so that we would have the energy and the acuity that our clients and each other would need. So, fairly sure this was going to be the beginning of a long haul—and it certainly turned out to be one!—we decided to get a full night's sleep and then come up with a plan for the pandemic: Personal High-Performance Practices.

The following day, we took twenty minutes to brainstorm the very best ways we knew to keep our performance optimal. We knew we would need to invest our time first into the actions that would take care of our capacity to stay sharp—and then on our work. Far from the "rise and grind" mantras that frequent some work cultures, we each took the time to really consider what recharged us, kept us grounded, and created a space for a personal reset. For me, the list looked like this:

- *Put your faith in God.*
- *Get a good workout in at least every other day.*
- *Get a good night's sleep (at least 7 hours).*
- *Invest time in study of the Bible.*
- *Read at least 1 hour of fiction.*

Because Julie, as one of the top speakers for young women and youth leaders in the world, is more extroverted than I am, she included on her list at #5 her "extrovert's bike ride." Every day at about 5 pm, she'd ride around the neighborhood, saying hello (from a safe distance) to everyone outside. I could literally see the difference in her tension before and after; she carried her shoulders more loosely, talked more slowly, and smiled more after her ride. After a few weeks, Julie noticed the difference her greetings so obviously made on others—rare moments of human connection in an environment of social distancing.

Julie and I printed our lists and posted them prominently on the steel doors of our refrigerator, so they were continuously in sight and in mind.

The actions on these lists may sound overly simple, inconsequential, or even frivolous, but they are not—they create the necessary conditions for enduring performance at the highest levels. They are both fuel and maintenance for me and therefore my coaching—and, when I do them, I am not only taking care of myself, but also my family and my clients. Together—and in whatever form they take for you as an individual—they comprise the secret to enduring high performance.

Because I work with many CEOs and senior leaders in large organizations, I knew the impact would only intensify. Over the coming weeks, it really did—CEOs asked me to join their crisis meetings to help their senior teams, then called me at night to walk them through the bigger picture—and sometimes their family concerns. More than one CEO and I were in contact almost daily. "What do we do?" and "How do we communicate to our people?" were constant questions we addressed together. In the scary and ambiguous pandemic environment that we all lived in, fear and frustration bred—and I was getting extra doses through supporting my clients in challenging and charged moments. Because I continued to invest time in working out, in sleeping, and in reading—even though there always seemed to be more to do—I made certain that I could serve everyone better.

Over the next few weeks, many of my clients created their own Personal High-Performance Practices—because they needed to be at their best for the people who counted on them. Here are just some examples from their lists:

- *One CEO began to audition hobbies, from bike-riding to solo soccer.*
- *The CFO of a software firm focused on the importance of a steady workout.*
- *The CHRO of a multi-billion-dollar retail company decided to keep an hour to herself in the morning for physical fitness and left her work smartphone in a drawer until she finished.*

- *The President of a $600M firm embraced clean eating and focused on being fully present during time with his family, especially his young granddaughter.*

Though simple, this idea isn't always easy because is seems to drive against the habit of action so common to successful people—I write "seems" because these lists comprise the strategically important actions that make a real difference in profound, sustainable, enjoyable success. It may require some support to accomplish at first. You might want an accountability partner. Several senior leaders made spreadsheets of the most important action items, so they could track their progress. As a coach to these senior leaders, I would follow up with them on the commitments they made to themselves.

Because of Personal High-Performance Practices, these leaders generated visible, crucially important outcomes for themselves and their companies. Among other outcomes, they:

Avoided burnout – Several senior leaders admitted they avoided a potential burnout and crash—great outcomes for them personally and their enterprises, which would have suffered greatly at losing their leadership during the crisis.

Enhanced leadership – Increased patience and resilience led to faster and more-effective decisions in a moment of crisis. In one specific example, this allowed one executive to better positively influence the crisis-response strategy and restructuring of a billion-dollar company.

Enhanced executive teamwork – One CEO noted better relationships with his executive team, resulting in better communication and quicker execution—as well as fewer missteps because of the communication.

Enhanced strategic thinking – Multiple leaders mentioned the ability to think more broadly and include more perspectives in their planning, leading to better-thought-out, more-flexible, more-innovative, and more-effective responses to a fast-moving crisis.

In virtually every case, you are the most important resource over which you have any control to benefit your life, your mission, and your company. No one ever argues that you shouldn't put gas in the company car. Most executives would discipline or maybe even fire a leader for failure to take appropriate care of capital equipment. In fact, many large manufacturing companies often shut down for a few days to a week each year to conduct maintenance because it means the rest of the year has higher production and fewer breakdowns. So, how can we as leaders recognize the same advantage ourselves?

If you are reading this book, you're clearly the kind of leader who cares deeply about delivering consistently high performance in your work and your life. So, like I ask the CEOs who work with me, ask yourself these questions:

What actions and activities refuel your performance most powerfully?

How often would it serve you to do them to be at your best, because you and your company deserve your best?

How will you track them?

With thoughtful answers, I'm certain that you, too, will be able to do less and get more done.

Bill Carrier, *President of Carrier Leadership Coaching Inc., coaches CEOs and senior executives. He is co-founder of The Future of Coaching magazine, a former Rotary International Ambassadorial Scholar to Brazil, and a graduate of The U.S. Military Academy at West Point.*

bill@carriercoaching.com

How to Lead When You're Feeling Afraid

By Peter Bregman, *Author | Speaker | Executive Coach | CEO at Bregman Partners, Inc.*

"There is no use trying," said Alice; "one can't believe impossible things." "I dare say you haven't had much practice," said the Queen. "When I was your age, I always did it for half an hour a day. Why, sometimes I've believed as many as six impossible things before breakfast."

Alice in Wonderland — Lewis Carroll

'd known Jeff (not his real name) for many years, as a client and as a friend, but I'd never seen him so thrown. I could feel his fear, his sense of uncertainty.

And it was with good reason.

Jeff was the head of sales for a company whose product was, more or less, impossible to sell.

His company, Golden Global (also not its real name), is an active fund manager. Active funds invest in particular stocks that they think will do well, as opposed to passive funds, which track an established index, such as the S&P 500. Today, many investors are pulling their money out of active funds and putting it into passive ones. In January 2017 alone, investors withdrew $13.6 billion from active funds and invested $77 billion in passive ones.

It makes sense: In addition to charging dramatically lower fees, passive has outperformed active 92% of the time over the past 15 years. Like the rest of the industry, Golden Global's fund performance has lagged.

Jeff was facing ridiculous odds even if his only goal was to keep cash from flowing out of Golden Global's investments. But that wasn't his goal. His goal was to increase total investment in Golden Global's strategic products — by $2 billion.

So, Jeff and his team were working harder than they ever had before, going to the clients they knew, making a case that had previously worked for their funds, selling their hearts out doing the things that they'd had success with in the past.

But it wasn't the past.

They were looking for their lost keys in the same pockets they'd checked again and again. Their frenzy of activity was getting them exactly nowhere.

Here's the dilemma: The only way you can solve an impossible challenge is through innovation and experimentation. But fear blocks innovation and experimentation. Meanwhile Jeff and his entire team were terrified. They feared falling short of their goal and losing their bonuses. Ultimately, they feared losing their jobs.

So, here's the question: How can you inspire your team to achieve the impossible when you yourself are feeling afraid and uncertain about how — and whether — you can achieve it?

When Jeff and I first spoke, he thought he had a sales problem. But that wasn't quite right. What Jeff really had was a leadership problem. He needed to inspire people to loosen up, try new things, experiment. He needed to get people thinking out of the box at the precise moment that they were huddling together in a small corner of it.

How do you get out of this conundrum?

Build Emotional Courage

Your first step is to build your emotional courage — your ability to act thoughtfully, strategically, and powerfully while feeling afraid.

Why not just overcome your fear? That's what most people try to do (and what many coaches and therapists try to help people do), but it's a huge mistake.

In our conversations, Jeff called himself a coward, but he couldn't have been more wrong. Jeff wasn't a coward. He was a normal person in a scary situation. Actually, he was an incredibly brave person in a scary situation. In other words, Jeff's fear was appropriate. So, not feeling the fear was not a smart, or realistic, option.

But he was overwhelmed by his fear, and it was driving him to push his people in a way that kept them smaller, taking fewer risks, and staying stuck — which is why emotional courage is so critical.

Jeff and I spent some time increasing his capacity to feel the fear without losing himself in it. I asked him where in his body he felt it. What did it feel like? Did it move? He felt it as a knot in his stomach, as a constriction in his throat, as a pain in his heart. We stayed with those feelings and watched them shift, move, lighten. He learned the critical skill of feeling the fear without becoming it.

At that point he could feel scared without acting scared. He wasn't ignoring his fear — he still felt scared — but it didn't control him. That was a critical move toward showing up as an inspirational leader.

Focus on the Process

We're often told (including by me) that we should focus on the outcomes we want to achieve (for example, driving to a sales target). And we should. Usually.

But when we're scared or intimidated or pursuing something so big that we don't even really know where to begin, we need to focus on the process that will get to the outcome. A good process will guide you along the path to get you where you want to go, and you can follow a good process no matter what you're feeling.

The next thing we did was shift Jeff's mindset from sell more to sell differently. Small change, massive shift.

"Sell more" is outcome-focused, while "sell differently" is process-focused. It answers the question: "What should I do, day in and day out, that will get me to that outcome?"

"Sell differently" was precisely the prompt that he and his people needed in order to redirect their energy from working harder to working more strategically.

Communicate Clearly

Once you bolster your emotional courage and target your focus, you need to direct the attention of your team.

Jeff had sent some emails that were meant to inspire but had the opposite effect. He basically kept telling people they needed to step it up, work harder, and be accountable (for example, sell more).

We asked the question:

How can he communicate, as a leader, in an environment of fear so that his people are inspired to seek creative solutions to a sticky, impossible problem?

After reading a number of his emails, I wrote out the simplest structure I could think of to redirect the energy of his communication, offering a four-part outline:

1. **Vision** – People need to have a clear sense of where they are headed. You should articulate the vision so that it's succinct, simple, palpable, and clear.

2. **Empathy** – People need to know that you are not out of touch and that you can feel what they are feeling. You do not need to drag this part out — it should be short, but connected and heartfelt. This is where you can also own your part in the challenge.

3. **Direction** – People need to see the path that they can believe will get them to the ultimate objective: the vision. Like the vision, your direction should be succinct, simple, palpable, and clear.

4. **Proof** – People need a reason to believe they can walk the path, so you should offer proof for your direction and optimism. You should be specific, be personal, and reflect the work that the team is already doing. This will build your team's confidence.

Here's one example of how it played out in Jeff's communication to his team:

"I am excited about what this business could look like when we share ideas and take some risks in selling differently. We do not need investors to put all their money with us — we need them to put a portion of their money with us, and it's a good idea for them to do it — we are an important part of a well-rounded portfolio, and we're good at what we do." (Vision)

"We obviously have serious product challenges. The outflows are disheartening. This is a scary time for all of us, and I realize that I have contributed to that in my own communications. I'm sorry for that." (Empathy)

"Doing things differently is our path to success, and it requires that we take some risks. Our opportunity is in expanding our client base, finding those who see our offerings as solutions to the exposure they have in the broader market, and sharing the compelling story we see. I don't have all the answers — but I believe in you, and together, we can make it happen." (Direction)

"There are already a lot of great ideas — and we've made tremendous progress — that show what we can do when we focus on taking risks and changing our approach. Some things I'm hearing include that Alex streamlined non-sales meetings and added one weekly sales meeting to share ideas. Danielle's team analyzed what had been successful, and it was a very high-touch sales process, which is hard with 200 clients per territory, so they narrowed it to 60. That's a big, risky change — which is precisely what we need to be doing. And when Michelle sees that a client doesn't understand the strategy, she shifts to education about the space rather than doubling down on the sale. This is just some of what I'm hearing, and it shows what we can do when we take risks to do things differently." (Proof)

Once you've got the four-part outline down, your job is to repeat it. All the time. Shifting behavior in others requires repetition. You may become bored with it — and you may feel that you're overdoing it — but use your newly developed emotional courage to feel those feelings and keep repeating yourself anyway.

The result? It's not over yet. But the changes that Jeff and his team were looking for have started in dramatic ways. Remember their "impossible" goal to increase total investment in Golden Global's strategic products by $2 billion? When we last spoke, they were already close to $1 billion.

Peter is the Founder and CEO of Bregman Partners. He is the bestselling author or contributor of 20 books, most recently, "You Can Change Other People." Peter is recognized as the #1 executive coach in the world and ranked as one of the Top 8 thought leaders in leadership by Thinkers50. He also leads the Bregman Leadership Intensive, ranked the #1 Leadership program in the world. He is host of the top 10 Business Podcast, Bregman Leadership Podcast.

https://www.bregmanpartners.com

Woman, CEO, Mother and Daughter:
From the Brink of Crisis to Unimagined Possibilities

By Jennifer McCollum, *CEO at Linkage Inc.*

"What is the truest, most beautiful life you can imagine? Tell the story and write it down. And remember: We can do hard things...but we can't do impossible things."
— Glennon Doyle at Linkage's Women in Leadership Institute, Nov 2020

As the world came to a halt in the spring of 2020, the constraints felt like shackles. At work, our business was paralyzed as we all tried desperately to determine the COVID impact on our employees and customers, and clients simultaneously canceled or postponed their work with us. Months of planned business travel, where I would be speaking on stages at conferences nationwide, slipped away quickly, one trip at a time. At home, my kids were abruptly pulled from school, while our counties nationwide struggled individually with how to pivot overnight into an impossible virtual-only environment.

My husband constructed a makeshift office in the dining room, and our three children roamed aimlessly from one room to another with their technology, trying to adjust to a new world with their social structures crumbling beneath them. We reassigned house chores and created new routines, centered around stay-at-home orders – cooking, sports, work, school, and entertainment. I felt an immense pressure to sort through all this and hold it together on all fronts, but the world was fragile... and I was too.

I am a woman, a mother, and an executive, and I have been constrained in the last year by the same things that many other women have faced – navigating a new work environment from home that is both virtual and never-ending, while still serving as a primary contributor of all non-paid work in the home – including childcare, housework, and managing aging parents. It's exhausting, and yet I fully acknowledge my privilege, with means to pay for additional support and a caring spouse who shares in the household tasks.

As the CEO of a company dedicated to changing the face of leadership, my vision is to advance women and other under-represented groups into leadership roles. I'm especially concerned now, because as bad as the health and economic crises have been for the entire workforce across genders and levels, we know it has been far worse for women. Decades of excruciatingly slow progress toward gender equity in leadership are now being reversed, as the ongoing public health crisis threatens one in four women who are considering opting out of the workforce altogether. Women are experiencing two times the burnout rate and are three times more likely to be sidelined in our careers due to the increasing demands of home and family life. It is more important than ever for our organizations – and all of us as leaders – to demonstrate a meaningful commitment to women leaders.

And knowing all this, I still feel the struggle, even more acutely in the swirl of a global pandemic. As the COVID constraints threatened to continue well beyond the spring into summer, fall, and winter, I continued to explore critical questions: How can I use these constraints to pivot, both for myself and my business? How can I better manage my work, my family, and my own wellbeing through seemingly impossible circumstances?

Looking at this year of crisis in retrospect, the struggle has also allowed a time of reflection, clarity, innovation, and deepening relationships. I slowly came to understand that the constraints of my new life also provided new possibilities, with boundaries to guide me forward creatively. The constraints helped me redefine my dreams and aspirations, both personally and professionally, allowing new opportunities to emerge as I was forced to slow down, listen, and engage differently with myself and others.

In our Linkage book, *Mastering Your Inner Critic and 7 Other High Hurdles to Advancement*, we teach women how to practice self-awareness to change what matters most to them. Through our 20 years of women's leadership assessment, development, and coaching, we uncovered what we call the Inner Critic and seven specific hurdles that women face as they rise in their careers. While difficult to observe or measure, these internal hurdles can hold us back in terms of progress toward our own advancement. In a world where some hurdles seemed insurmountable, continued focus on identifying and scaling them helped me to find some freedom within the constraints I felt.

The Inner Critic – How do we quiet the voice in our head that expresses judgment of us and others? This is the ultimate and uber hurdle, which is always present and weaves its way throughout all the others. It's the voice that tells us we aren't good enough, or we shouldn't speak up in a meeting because we won't add value, or we aren't really qualified for our job, especially given the extraordinary demands of life in a pandemic.

As I took on more of the housework, cooking, dog-walking, and online schooling, all while trying to manage layoffs, redefine our strategy, and engage the remaining staff, I found myself questioning whether I had the energy and capability to meet this challenge. I paused and noticed that I was sad, anxious, and even angry at how my year had turned so rapidly. I tried to become more compassionate with myself – and my team and family – acknowledging the fear and uncertainty. I wasn't operating at my best, but nobody else was either.

Bias – What are deeply held beliefs that no longer serve us? As we got deeper into COVID, I became more aware of many beliefs that I could examine and even release, like:

- *I need to "hold it all together" for my staff and for my family.*
- *I have to orchestrate all the household activities, or they won't get done.*
- *I can't lead the company through this crisis and be available for my family.*

In fact, this crisis allowed me more time and energy to focus on how I wanted to show up as a leader at work and at home. I could engage more authentically, as we all did the best we could, working with technology lapses, kids and dogs in the background, and work-from-video attire. I observed my husband start walking the dog and cooking, because my work meetings would often start earlier and end later than his. I admired the kids as they figured out how to navigate school and social relationships, while adjusting to unimaginable losses for them – prom, sports championships, graduation, college visits, and more. It is only in retrospect that I realize these biases began to dissipate due to the constraints of our new at-home lives, and the people closest to me shifted their behaviors as a result.

Clarity – How do we tap into our passion, our values, and our dreams and create intention about our future and professional advancement? During the worst financial year of my professional career, the most important thing to me was to stabilize the company and put a better plan in place so we could thrive as the COVID cloud lifted. At the same time, I was focused on the mental health and safety of my family and my own parents. I realized I didn't want to lose the clarity I had about my own development and aspirations to evolve into more big-stage speaking and writing, and to support the evolution of Linkage's brand externally.

I mourned the loss of my plans, but as the year progressed, I found other ways to achieve those goals – as a guest on podcasts and countless virtual events, including our very own Women in Leadership Institute where 1,500 women joined on an immersive and innovative platform. The constraints created new opportunities to achieve the same outcome, and no one could tell I was broadcasting in my slippers from my home office.

Proving our value – How do we stop doing so much? This is the hurdle that has plagued me most of my life, with the mistaken belief that if I do it myself, it will be "better," and I will be recognized and rewarded for my job well done. As we rise as leaders – especially women leaders – it becomes more important to inspire others to do work aligned with their strengths, and not do it ourselves. As a CEO, my job is more often allocating work to teams and then stepping out of the way.

However, as the company and the world fell apart rapidly, that felt like a scary and ill-advised way to manage. I found myself diving deeply into many workstreams, to figure out alongside my executive team how to respond urgently. That lasted for several months and many sleepless nights, but once we emerged with a "better plan" to respond to the changing environment, I tried to shift my focus to areas where I could uniquely contribute, like Board engagement, new-content partnerships, and distribution models. The team often does its best work when I'm encouraging from the sidelines versus inserting myself in the game. Ironically, the family does too.

Recognized confidence – How do we embrace our own wisdom, strength, and power? This isn't about worthiness, but operating with confidence, even when our inner critic is activated and imposter syndrome kicks in. I have never been a big champion of "fake it till you make it," as it feels disingenuous. However, when my confidence was rattled across the last year, I leaned on my advisors, peers, and friends to remind me that I was enough, just as I was, and my experiences – combined with data and intuition – would help me stand tall and lead through the crisis, even during the many times when I was unsure of myself.

Branding & presence – How do we show up in a way that we wish to be known for? Since taking on my latest role nearly three years ago, I had clarity about building a brand as an inspiring, authentic, visionary CEO known for leading business transformation, thought leadership, and product innovation. As the crisis unfolded, I sought opportunities to demonstrate those aspirations in public and private forums with current and potential clients, business partners, and investors.

Making the ask – How do we ask for what we really want? The constraints of our new home and work life allowed for near-constant requests and negotiation. I made asks of my husband and children about shifting responsibilities around the much higher degree of housework needed with all of us working, studying, and eating at home. At work, I made asks of our staff and our Board, which required great sacrifice for all of us in the form of financials, work hours, flexibility, and job rescoping. As I worked with the women on my team, I became clearer and coached them on what asks were appropriate and accessible in a crisis – like reducing workload expectations or shifting work hours – as opposed with asks that were not appropriate given the environment – like salary increases.

Networking – How do we build stronger relationships that in turn make us stronger? Given the all-virtual format our lives have become at work, networking became a bigger opportunity and need. To explore rapidly how to pivot and innovate our entire business, I shifted immediately to engaging and expanding my external network, dedicating about 40% of my time to these efforts. As a newer member of the Marshall Goldsmith 100 Coaches, I accessed dozens of inspiring world-changers with specific offers and requests. Whether in groups or individually, we impacted each other personally and professionally. This was probably the single reason I emerged from the constraints of the year in a much better position, and it took scaling every other hurdle – quieting my inner critic, overcoming my biases, gaining clarity and confidence, articulating my brand and showing up consistently, and making specific asks.

As our staff and I rallied around our long-term mission to "Change the Face of Leadership" and our short-term intention to survive the year, we were energized and committed to innovation and reinvention of the company. We relentlessly pursued our revised goals amid incredible adversity. The constraints of the year brought our lives and our business to a temporary crash, but also gave us urgency to innovate and pivot, both about who we are as individuals and as an organization. Not one person left the firm voluntarily, and our future looks brighter than it might have before COVID disrupted life as we knew it...and will likely not know it again.

Jennifer McCollum is CEO of Linkage, where she oversees the strategic direction and global operations of the Boston–based leadership development firm. Through work with more than one million leaders, Linkage empowers leading organizations globally to advance women and create inclusive leaders and organizations.

She lives in the Washington, D.C., area with her husband and three kids, and enjoys tennis, skiing, and morning lattes. She has a master's degree in communications from the University of Stirling in Stirling, Scotland, and an undergraduate degree from Wake Forest University.

https://www.linkageinc.com/team-member/jennifer-mccollum/

Put on
Your Own
Oxygen Mask
First

S elfcare is always important, and I love the take our experts have when they show how investing in your own emotional and physical health is key to surviving and thriving the challenges that life throws your way. Many people underestimate the importance of good health in being able to handle obstacles. This section addresses the ways in which you need to care for yourself when under pressure or when you feel a loss of control from an unforeseen roadblock. What follows are ways to connect, stay real, be personal, and expand your reach to contribute to wellbeing in today's digital world and in a Covid-19 world where it has not been possible for as much direct human connection and interaction as we would have liked.

Health First

By Julie Rosenberg, MD, *Senior Consultant and Author*

"There's nothing more important than our good health – that's our principal capital asset."
— Arlen Specter

The year 2020 was like none that had come before. A new strain of coronavirus, SARS-CoV-2, swept the globe, leaving a broad swath of death and devastation in its wake. America faced an unprecedented convergence of events — a global pandemic, a nation on the brink of recession, and a racial reckoning taking place across the country — and saw infection rates skyrocket while politicians argued about the utility of facemasks.

As the pandemic ravaged the country, many businesses closed. When they slowly began reopening their doors, organizational leaders sought guidance from a variety of sources and circulated lengthy protocol lists ranging from hand-sanitization stations to temperature checks to wearing facemasks at work.

The pandemic highlighted one truth that I have emphasized throughout my medical career — the single most important element of any company is the health and wellbeing of its employees. In this chapter, I argue that we maximize wellness at work by reframing self-care as the first step in our approach to the modern workplace.

For years now, we have understood the relationship of health in the workplace to the health of a company's bottom line. From 2010 to 2018, the corporate wellness industry in the United States tripled in size to $8 billion, coming to encompass more than 50 million American workers.[3] Yet there emerged a great irony — during an era in which everyone has been increasingly focused on wellness, it is painfully clear that we are

[3] Per "What Do Workplace Wellness Programs Do? Evidence from the Illinois Workplace Wellness Study." The University of Chicago, June 2018.

becoming less and less well as people. The majority of employees are over-tired, stressed out, disengaged, and disenchanted, and yet fear repercussions for taking an occasional "mental health" or personal day. And this was our condition before the pandemic.

Work and wellbeing are strongly linked and must be addressed together. The pandemic has given us an impetus to redefine norms and guidelines within organizations, starting at the very top. We must take a close look at existing wellness initiatives and reframe how companies might better support employees in the here and now, as it has been clearly shown that wellness programs don't work.[4]

Focus on self-care

We are burnt out as a society — a condition that goes well beyond fatigue. Burnout is characterized by a chronic state of emotional, physical, and mental exhaustion, accompanied by strong feelings of frustration and powerlessness. Burnout is caused by excessive and prolonged stress and is a condition of the modern workplace — and we were functioning that way well before the pandemic occurred. The SARS-CoV2 pandemic merely exacerbated our previous state.

Given the realities of society today, the issue of health in the workplace is more urgent than ever. In order to center the focus on health and wellbeing at work, we must first remove the stigma around taking care of ourselves. We have an impression in our society that self-care means candles and bubble baths. Self-care is not selfish. We cannot serve others well unless we take care of ourselves.

Self-care begins by asking ourselves what we need — emotionally, spiritually, physically — at any given moment. Self-care includes focusing on what we eat, how much we're sleeping, whether we get daily exercise, whether we incorporate practices such as yoga and meditation into our lives (both of which are proven stress relievers, as has been

[4] Johnson, Steven Ross. "Workplace wellness programs don't improve employee health: study." Modern Healthcare, April 16, 2019.

shown in scientific literature).[5] A focus on self-care is the wellspring of wellness, and it is a critical component of promoting good health.

By incorporating simple lifestyle changes, we can support a lifelong approach to wellbeing. Three key aspects of self-care are below.

Move Your Body

I have always found that the more I move, the better my day is. I typically start my day with about an hour of movement, doing some cardio and weights, an online yoga class, or outdoor cycling; these daily workouts have helped me to be more engaged, alert, focused, and productive at work.

While a morning workout may not resonate for you, it's important to move your body! Many of us have been homebound for months, without our usual routines and with unforeseen hardships. This has led to a vulnerability to overeating, sedentary behavior, and weight gain (aka the "Quarantine 15"). Movement is key to our health and longevity. We must not emerge from the pandemic with more obesity, more cardiovascular disease, and more sedentary lifestyles.

One key to improving a "lifestyle lapse" in movement is to come up with a plan. If you are unable to continue your usual gym session or exercise classes, commit now to other forms of daily activity, such as walking or hiking outdoors or participating in online fitness or yoga classes.

Still Your Mind

The soundtrack of our lives is a cacophony of alerts — text messages, push notifications, and breaking news. We are poised to answer an urgent email from our boss or a client at all hours of the day and night. In addition, we shift endlessly from task to task in an effort to create more time and opportunity for ourselves. Perhaps we don't realize that when we multi-task, we fracture our concentration. We do more things, but we do them less well, and, most likely, only partially complete them.

[5] B. Rael Cahn, Matthew S. Goodman, Christine T. Peterson, Raj Maturi, Paul J. Mills. "Yoga, Meditation and Mind-Body Health: Increased BDNF, Cortisol Awakening Response, and Altered Inflammatory Marker Expression after a 3-Month Yoga and Meditation Retreat." Frontiers in Human Neuroscience, August 22, 2017.

People who try to do too much all at once will most often find themselves less productive and less efficient. This sense of constant distraction is intensified by our increasingly uncertain world. Today we worry not only about meeting a major deadline but also about the threats of infection, job loss, and financial instability. Collectively, this all can lead to excessive stress and anxiety that impact our lives in negative ways.

How can we shield ourselves from massive information overwhelm and retrain our minds along an intentional path? Here are two simple tips: 1) Start each morning intentionally without checking email and text messages the moment you wake up. 2) Make time each day for quietude and reflection. One way to do so is to use breathing and centering techniques in small increments throughout each day. For example, try "square breathing" — breathe in for a count of four, hold for a count of four, exhale for a count of four, and then pause for a count of four. This breathing pattern takes just a few minutes and will help you to relax and ease your mind.

Feed Yourself

The adage "you are what you eat" has been around for ages because of a simple fact: It's true. What we put in our bodies has a direct impact on how we feel and how we function. For us to be truly well, we must first make a commitment to feeding ourselves what we need — and "feeding" includes everything we are giving ourselves and our bodies, from healthy and nutritious foods that boost our immune system to quality sleep.

Stressful and uncertain times can significantly change how we eat, as we tend to crave higher-fat and higher-sugar foods, and to eat when we aren't necessarily hungry. What we put into our bodies has an enormous — and immediate — impact on how we function. Many of us eat an abundance of processed foods, which are chemical-laden addictive foods usually sold in jars, boxes, and bags. These products may taste good, but they are often filled with saturated fat and sugar and stripped of nutrients.

We can confront our uncertain world by eating a diet replete with high-quality, unrefined, and minimally processed foods such as vegetables and fruits, whole grains, healthy fats, and good sources of protein. Eating a whole foods and nutritious diet on a regular schedule will stabilize your blood sugar and help you to avoid many of the ups and downs that you might experience during the day.

What we feed our minds is also essential. Are you careful about what kinds of information you're regularly feeding on, or do you simply ingest whatever comes your way? We are often overwhelmed by negative news and negative thoughts — both our own and those from others. We must be careful about the information we allow to enter our minds. We must also proactively feed and exercise our brains by training, expanding, or challenging our minds. Learn a new skill. Read a book.

Tackle a crossword puzzle each week.

Last, feeding ourselves with quality sleep is essential. Healthy adults need between seven and nine hours of sleep per night for optimal functioning. This amount of sleep is not always easy to get after a stressful day balancing life and work. Here's a tip: To relax and achieve restful sleep, turn off all electronic media a minimum of 90 minutes before going to bed.

In summary, the pandemic upended life as we know it and reminded us that health is our first and foremost priority. Wellbeing starts with the individual. We are each responsible and accountable for our own life. By incorporating simple lifestyle changes, we can develop a lifelong approach to wellbeing and a more agile and effective approach to work.

Julie Rosenberg, M.D., is a Pharmaceutical Consultant and Executive Advisor. She is passionate about helping leaders to become more resilient by adopting healthy lifestyles and living with intention. Dr. Rosenberg is the author of two books: Beyond the Mat: Achieve Focus, Presence and Enlightened Leadership Through the Principles and Practice of Yoga and Be True: A Personal Guide to Becoming Your Most Authentic Self. She writes a weekly column for the Island Sun entitled Health First.

http://www.drjulierosenberg.com

Turn on a Dime? Not So Fast!

By Sally Helgesen, *Author, How Women Rise, The Female Vision, The Web of Inclusion*

"The best way to predict the future is to create it."
— Peter Drucker

Until March 10, 2020, I had typically spent 45 weeks a year on the road. Making ceaseless presentations to clients on topics that passionately engaged me was exhilarating and exhausting. I prided myself on my road warrior ethic and found refreshment in spontaneous encounters in odd corners of the world: wide-ranging conversations, warm embraces, "let's keep in touch" goodbyes.

Then, within the space of a week, my entire year of work was cancelled, and I found myself unexpectedly and relentlessly at home. And while I was glad to no longer be a body hurtling through space – which is how I often imagined myself – I had suddenly lost my primary source of income, satisfaction, and joy. And I had no idea what might replace it.

Colleagues advised that I waste no time in reconfiguring my work – and, it seemed, my entire being. I remember one well-intentioned soul importuning me to follow his lead and turn myself into a hologram that clients could download. Another urged that I find a partner who could quickly turn my life's work into phone-accessible apps.

I appreciated the kind intentions, but it all felt a bit absurd. We were in the midst of a pandemic that was killing people. Three jazz musicians I'd known for decades were among the early dead. Friends were stranded in Mexico, Brazil, the Italian Alps. On a mundane level, we were baffled about how to acquire basic necessities in an era of empty shelves amid warnings that a grocery trip could land us in the ICU. As my husband focused on securing hand sanitizer and masks online and decontaminating groceries and mail in our garage, the prospect of seamlessly reinventing myself – "pivoting on a dime" was the phrase I kept hearing – seemed a form of denial.

I decided that I needed instead to deal with the enormity of what was happening, to take time to reflect on what might be next. I was aided in this by some timely counsel I'd received from Marshall Goldsmith days before the shutdown, when we delivered an International Women's Day program at eBay together. Elbow-bumping our goodbyes as we left for our respective airports, Marshall said, "This is going to be a tough road. We don't know what's coming or when we'll be able to work again. My advice is simple. Use your time to build your brand, stay connected, and be real."

When I was safely home, Marshall's words spurred me to be intentional about addressing my situation in a way that offered scope to adjust. Because lockdown felt isolating and disorienting, I decided to start with his injunction to stay connected.

I resolved to give myself one full month to reach out on a fulltime basis.

I then began making long lists of people to call or email: extended family, friends of family, my broad network of colleagues, longtime friends and recent friends, people I'd worked with over the last 10 or 20 years, old classmates, neighbors, former neighbors, service people on whose support I had depended.

The pandemic meant that I didn't need to start these conversations with excuses about why I hadn't been in touch or explanations about why I was reaching out now. I stuck to the basics: How are you? What's it like for your family? Are you feeling okay? Did you lose your work? I also kept it personal – no group emails, no social media blasts, no "dear friends" announcements. My goal was to connect from the heart in a time of turmoil, which meant doing so from a point of shared vulnerability and fear of an uncertain future.

Once I felt more rooted in my extended community, I turned my attention to building my brand. In the early stages of the pandemic, this basically meant doing a lot of free work, work that brought me no income (there was almost none to be had in those first months) but would raise awareness about what I have to contribute.

Like most of my colleagues in the leadership field, I'm routinely inundated with requests for unpaid work: webinars, podcasts, short articles, guest appearances in college classes, live programs for nonprofits and professional networks with tiny budgets. I've always been grateful for these invitations but was rarely able to accept them because I was slammed with lucrative speaking engagements that kept me flying around the globe.

Now that I was going nowhere and the work could all be done from my home office, I started saying yes, fairly indiscriminately at first. Soon I was connecting with audiences in Sao Paulo and Cork, Mumbai and Seoul, Lagos and Moscow, Nairobi and Warsaw – as well as all over the U.S. and Canada – sometimes within the same day.

This proved valuable in many ways. First, I was able to reach far more people than usual because the events required no travel or hotel time. This accessibility enabled me to raise my profile on an unprecedented scale and reach large groups I never could have in the past. I also got a crash course on how to deliver programs virtually with skill and passion. The sheer volume of engagements gave me lots of opportunities to learn, often by making mistakes. Since I wasn't being paid, it was a lot easier to let it go when I messed up.

All this brand-building paradoxically supported the third part of Marshall's injunction, using this strange time to "be real." I'd assumed that having my work mediated by technology would make it feel less personal than live appearances, especially since I wouldn't be having the kind of spontaneous interactions with participants and clients that make the before-and-after of in-person events so satisfying. But I found just the opposite to be true. Total immersion showed me that virtual platforms did, in fact, offer many advantages when it came to establishing a personal bond with an audience.

By erasing so many distractions – body language, the hierarchy of where people sit, the size of the stage, the speaker's distance from participants, awkward acoustics, depressing venues, painful shoes – platforms like Zoom and WebEx focus unprecedented attention on the connection between speaker and audience.

Having your face fill the entire screen creates a surprising kind of intimacy, the very last thing I had expected. I discerned this right away in the messages I got from people after I delivered a presentation. "I feel as if I really know you"; "I feel as if you and I are best friends." These were different from the responses I'd gotten after speaking onstage. People were enthusiastic and often told me that they loved my message, but rarely expressed the belief that we had become intimate friends.

Of course, I had to learn to get comfortable with the intensity of this kind of attention. With the camera on my face, I had nowhere to hide. I couldn't shift my eyes away without breaking the bond that is the platform's strength. I had to relax into the moment and accept the intimacy. Being up close lets people read your heart, so I found myself consciously trying to connect with what the individuals who comprised my audiences were living through: worries about sick parents, possible layoffs, who would take care of the kids.

I kept this awareness front and center and let it shape how I spoke. I tried to feel the people in my audiences in my heart. Doing so made it clear that sharing some grand theory or leadership "model" wasn't going to cut it. Nor could I indulge in motivational fluff or lean too heavily on the crutch of research. I had to keep it real, which meant I had to be as practical and tactical as possible. I had to make my work all about them.

So the constraints of the pandemic created the conditions for a new and ultimately more rewarding relationship with my work. I experienced a sense of connectedness that had eluded me when my days vacillated between big staged events and lonely overnights in an Emirates lounge. I found fresh sources of support and inspiration. My work became less about my ideas and more about how people could use these ideas to have better lives.

This shift served me remarkably well when we got into the summer and clients began facing the fact that they weren't going to be rescheduling in-person events anytime soon. Because I'd taken my time, I felt prepared, experienced, and confident, and full of animating purpose. The result? Clients new and old rushed to get in touch.

One year later, I'm astonished at how fruitful Marshall's little mantra has been. It worked because it made sense, was simple to act on, and gave me permission to find my own way. I'm well into recovery now, and mindful of all the loss, still able to regard this very painful time as a gift.

Sally Helgesen, cited in Forbes as the world's premier expert on women's leadership, is an internationally bestselling author, speaker, and leadership coach. She is ranked number 6 among the world's top 30 leadership thinkers by Global Gurus and number one coach for women leaders by Thinkers50/100 Coaches.

Sally's most recent book, "How Women Rise," co-authored with Marshall Goldsmith, has been translated into 17 languages. Previous books include "The Female Advantage," "The Female Vision," and "The Web of Inclusion," cited in The Wall Street Journal as one of the best books on leadership of all time.

sally@sallyhelgesen.com

Finding Purpose in a Pandemic

By Tom Kolditz, PhD, *Founding Director, Ann & John Doerr Institute for New Leaders*

"Success without fulfillment is the ultimate failure."
— Richard Leider

For most of us who coach or do leader development work as our primary employment, the term "knowledge worker" fits. For knowledge workers, the constraints of COVID-19 restrictions have impacted calendars by changing the patterns of our work schedules. For example, according to research done by the calendar optimization company Clockwise, workers are spending an extra 60 to 90 minutes per week in team-sync meetings and are having 24% more time in one-on-one meetings, coupled with a 45% decrease in out-of-office events. At the same time, commuting by public transportation or private automobile has plummeted, giving back some of the time consumed by altered communication patterns.

Constraints often hold the keys to new insights. Recently a coaching client and I discussed how little we had traveled by commercial air during the pandemic, and guessed that we would never return to the travel tempo we once had. But then the conversation deepened into how creatively stimulating we both found airport environments to be. People on the move, motion, energy, the regulars, the first-timers, first class, no class, a hive of people watching people—there is something we both recognized in the travel environment that made us long for 45 minutes of concourse time. We remembered breakthrough innovations and forward-looking ideas, gate-spawned, rapidly thumbed through a device to colleagues and assistants. We will never forget that airports can be much more than places to board a plane.

While the pandemic may have suspended our airport musings, it has created other opportunities for thoughtful discussion as well. A friend

I had not spoken to in 15 years reached out to me for a call; I'll call him Bill. Bill was a former Army colonel and had a successful 25-year post-military career doing leader development work in two top global consulting firms. The pandemic made him focus on change in his professional life, and he had been invited by a mentor to become a coach with the mentor's small firm. The mentor, a retired general officer and octogenarian, said that coaching, mentoring, and advising people in business was easy. Bill, a thoughtful, intelligent, analytical person, wanted to know more about coaching, and I could tell by three minutes into the conversation that he was earnest, and taking careful notes as we spoke.

It was clear from the start of our discussion that Bill really didn't understand the fundamentals of coaching. As many other coaches have explained to the uninformed, coaching is vastly different from mentoring, where a person of greater experience shares knowledge and networks with a person more professionally junior. Bill needed to understand how coaching was different from the consulting work he had engaged in for most of his professional life. Coaching was unique, I explained, in that coaches don't have to be experts in their clients' fields, like mentors and consultants usually are. Instead, coaches use their skills to help their clients come to their own conclusions about goal setting and strategies for achieving those goals. Coaches shape clients cognitively, emotionally, and behaviorally, in directions important to the client, and chosen by the client, not the coach.

Bill was listening intently; I could hear him taking notes, and his repeated affirmations told me that he was following the conversation handily. I transitioned to an explanation of the multiple options for acquiring coaching skills through formal training, and named seven or eight popular coach training courses, both independent and university-hosted. We discussed coaching certifications, whether they were necessary for coaching, and which certifications were most prestigious. Bill is so heavily networked that we didn't need to spend much time on finding clients—though I explained the significant role Chief Human Resource

Officers often play in the establishment of coaching relationships. And then we came to the question that put the discussion on pause:

"Why do you want to coach people?"

It was one of those moments when a person opens their mouth and takes a breath to speak, but stops abruptly when they realize that they are not ready to press "Play." He could not articulate why he wanted to coach people. Trying to regain his footing on the question, he walked through why he thought he did consulting work—good pay, prestige, expert recognition, seeing his advice followed through to success. But at this point in his life, he no longer needed pay, coaching didn't seem to garner prestige or expert recognition, and he was now aware that coaches are usually not in the habit of dispensing advice. The conversation turned to the notion of purpose—a topic with which this highly successful executive was not personally familiar.

Finding one's purpose in work has gotten attention lately, particularly in leader development initiatives. Thought leader Richard Leider develops executives who are transitioning out of their traditional roles into work that gives them more joy, and has them consider the relationship among their gifts, passions, and values to determine their purpose. Fortune's CONNECT online leader development platform, for example, has a multisession workshop on purposeful leadership. MG100 member Jennifer McCollum is the CEO of Linkage, Inc., where she discovered that companies that develop leaders who do things for a purpose and with a purpose enjoy 2x stronger revenue growth, 4x profit growth, and 9x employee engagement. Thus, my question to Bill, and now to readers, "Why do you want to coach people?" is fundamental, relevant, and important.

There are a number of ways to get in touch with one's purpose, but what is consistent is that purpose is moderated by one's values. For example, some coaches find it purposeful to work with the most senior executives possible, because they value the impact that their work has at the highest level of companies. Other coaches see a senior executive focus as needlessly benefitting the top 1/2 of 1% of the most privileged people in the world, and thus build their coaching practice around more junior leaders, middle management, coaching teams, or other areas of focus. Both are manifesting their values in their work. Neither is more legitimate than the other. Both can fulfill their purpose. Values come first.

Bill and I concluded our call without determining his purpose, or fully understanding why he wanted to be a coach. He did, however, seem earnestly and passionately focused on developing a sense of his purpose as a part of his transformation, and coming to grips with the values that drove him. Whether or not you are a coach—are your gifts, passions, and values interacting in ways that call you to your work? And if you are a coach, why? Take some time to reflect, and be purposeful in your coaching and in all you do, especially insofar as COVID has shown us that life is fleeting. Make it meaningful.

Tom Kolditz is the Director, Doerr Institute for New Leaders at Rice University, named top university program by the Association of Leadership Educators. A retired Army brigadier general holding a PhD in Psychology, he received the Warren Bennis Award for Excellence in Leadership in 2017, and has ranked among the top 25 global coaches for three years. His life's purpose is to improve society by developing more and better leaders.

leadership@rice.edu , kolditzt@gmail.com

From Victim to Victory
Pandemic-Inspired Lessons in Personal Growth

By Anna Yusim, MD / Board-Certified Psychiatrist

"Leaving behind nights of terror and fear, I rise into a daybreak that's wondrously clear, I rise"
— Maya Angelou, Still I Rise

The wise words of philosopher Heraclitus remind us that "the only constant is change." In a year filled with great change, uncertainly, complexity, and tragedy for so many, we have been forced to dig deep and either discover or resurrect our internal reservoirs of strength, courage, and wisdom.

One of life's fundamental truths is that one day we will all experience pain that will bring us to our knees. When this happens, we may question if we are strong enough to withstand the challenge. We may cling to memories of the life we once had. We may wonder if the darkness will ever give way to light once again.

Unbearable pain, whether in the form of sadness, grief, loss, failure, abandonment, depression, or something else entirely, is an inevitable part of life. The question is not whether you too will be afflicted; the question is what to do when life brings you to your knees.

The year 2020, forever immortalized as the fateful year of the COVID-19 pandemic, brought many of us to our knees. It was a year that put into question our fundamental sense of safety, peace, and security while boldly highlighting the fragility of life. The word "privilege" became redefined, as many of those privileges we never thought of as privileges were suddenly and unexpectedly stripped away: being able to walk safely down the street without a mask, riding the subway, going out to restaurants, inviting friends over, and being able shrug nonchalantly at flu-like symptoms.

A challenge to our mental health

As a Manhattan psychiatrist, I have seen firsthand the mental health effects this pandemic has had on my patients, friends, family, and community. From a mental health standpoint, rates of anxiety, depression, and substance abuse soared during 2020, as did thoughts of suicide. In a study carried out by the Center for Disease Control and Prevention, 26% of individuals aged 18-24 have seriously considered suicide in the past 30 days. Frontline workers were particularly affected, especially at the beginning of the pandemic, having to put their lives on the line daily without proper personal protective equipment (PPE), resulting in many unnecessary deaths.

Social isolation and loneliness only exacerbated these feelings of depression and alienation, particularly in the elderly. COVID-19 evaded many standard medical treatments, leaving many doctors to tell their patients things like "just rest and let your body fight it," as patients became weaker and more oxygen-deprived with the passing days. For those whose bodies effectively fought the virus, many had long-term effects, ranging from temporary loss of smell and taste to longer-term brain fog, neurological symptoms, immune dysfunction, and even new-onset psychosis.

The effect on one's financial situation was equally devastating. Many managed to stay healthy, while being forced to watch the decline of their business and finances. Some did not know where their next rent payment would come from, fearing eviction for themselves and their families. Some dipped into their retirement savings, only to deplete them completely when they were still unemployed months later.

Despite the incredible challenges posed to us in 2020, it was also a year in which I witnessed a great number of my patients, family, friends, and colleagues evolve, grow, and transform in miraculous and unprecedented ways. Many rose to meet the challenge with a strength they didn't know they possessed. Until now.

The important question then becomes, "What enabled certain people to make lemonade out of lemons, salsa out of the rotten tomatoes, and tears of joy out of the painful cries?"

We are not victims here

Why is it that two people can suffer similar incidents of indescribable pain, yet one will recover quickly while the other will sink into the depths of despair? Why do some people demonstrate consistent resilience in the face of pain and adversity, while others adopt the righteous indignation of victimhood? Are they weaker in mind and spirit? Or do they unconsciously adopt a victim mentality without even realizing they have given up their authentic personal power?

While overcoming pain and dealing with life challenges are natural parts of life, experiencing a calamity or even suffering a tremendous hardship is very different from adopting a "victim mentality." The idea of playing the victim began with the biblical story of Genesis. Adam said, "I didn't do it. She told me to do it." Eve said, "I didn't do it. The snake made me do it." From this point in time, humanity stepped onto the wheel of blame, which has been turning ever since.

What does it mean to play the victim? Rather than acknowledge our role in creating our own lives, sometimes it can be much easier to blame our problems on an inept government, an unjust world, or a deadly virus. I do not at all mean to imply that these three "perpetrators" do not present very real challenges. Disease, mental health crises, poverty, discrimination, homelessness, hunger, and domestic abuse are just a few of the real and impactful human problems that became worse during COVID and that require widespread change at the social and global level. So how do we respond in the most constructive and empowering way? Do we lament these hardships or do we do something about it? Do we succumb to "woe is me," or do we commit to changing what we can control?

It is not uncommon to relish the feeling of righteous indignation that comes from being a victim. Over time, our grip on this role can grow so tight that we come to identify with it. For example, it becomes familiar to say "this always happens to me" when faced with adversity. We then become confused in thinking that we are primarily victims of our circumstances rather than creators of our destiny.

Taking back our power

Adopting a victim mentality is one of the primary ways we as human beings give away our power. While we frequently cannot control the life challenges and circumstances that befall us, with the pandemic being a perfect example, we do have control over how we view the situation and the mindset we adopt moving forward. A victim mentality can keep us stuck in a toxic, self-righteous state of pain, resentment, and indignation. Psychologically, it is one of the most disempowering roles we can adopt.

Blaming others can be far more comfortable than noticing the ways that we ourselves are responsible for our lives. For people who play the blame game, point fingers, and choose to remain the victim, the powerful decision of defining who they are belongs to the perpetrator and the circumstances that surround them.

But we are only victims for as long as we choose to be. The decision to learn from pain, suffering, and loss is up to us. By taking responsibility for all aspects of our lives, especially our attitudes, we can rise above our victim mentality.

When it comes to relinquishing our victim mentality, the most important steps are to recognize the control we have over the situation, externally and internally. Externally, this means taking the steps necessary to change our circumstances: wearing masks, keeping our families safe, helping those less fortunate, taking concrete steps to end injustice as we perceive it, to name just a few. Recognizing our agency in how we respond to our circumstances and becoming involved as an agent of change in our own lives as well as socially and globally can be incredibly empowering. This is one of the first steps to relinquishing our victim mentality.

Owning our thoughts

Taking responsibility for our thoughts and attitudes is equally empowering. Our minds are inherently far more powerful than we realize—powerful enough to create our life experience. In this way, our thoughts and emotions hold tremendous energy. Often what we hold in our hearts and minds colors our entire world. For this reason, harnessing the power of our thoughts is an important way of rising above a victim mentality. Even in the direst of circumstances, we must do our best to remain optimistic, finding the silver lining, and never losing hope. As Viennese psychiatrist and Holocaust survivor Dr. Viktor Frankl powerfully wrote, "in the concentration camp where all external freedoms were stripped away...no one can control what we think in our minds."

Interestingly, most of our lives are created by thoughts that are completely unconscious to us. This is why becoming aware of the automatic thoughts that derail us into pessimism and catastrophizing is so important. To be clear, the goal is not to eliminate negative thoughts, but to become more aware of them, accept them as a part of who we are, and in the process, gain greater control over them. In order to gain control over a victim mentality, we must become disciplined in not succumbing to excessive negative thinking. This principle is espoused in the words of Mahatma Gandhi, when he wrote, "I will not let anyone walk through my mind with their dirty feet."

Letting go of a victim mentality is not easy. It takes strength, courage, intention, discipline, and sometimes faith. The atrocities experienced by many from COVID, both individually and collectively, not only cause us pain, but they shake our sense of security and can deeply wound our pride. They can feel intensely personal, and it's hard to let them go. But if we don't let them go, they stay stuck in the recesses of our minds and hearts for years, draining our energy without our even knowing it.

By learning to take responsibility for our attitudes and our own thoughts, we can take valuable steps towards relinquishing a victim mentality. It is up to us to harness our own power so we can make the most important changes in living fulfilled lives under any circumstances.

Dr. Anna Yusim *is an award-winning, Stanford- and Yale-educated, Board Certified Psychiatrist and executive coach with a robust private practice in New York City and Connecticut. On the Clinical Faculty at Yale Medical School, Dr. Yusim is internationally recognized as a trailblazer among healers, a gifted speaker, and the bestselling author of "Fulfilled: How the Science of Spirituality Can Help You Live a Happier, More Meaningful Life."*

https://www.annayusim.com/

Keeping
the Wheels On

The authors share their subject matter expertise along with lessons learned in addressing a variety of business-related challenges. They provide a varied set of building blocks that anyone can use to create value, grow their business, and increase employee engagement. The authors highlight how constraints provided direction and enhanced clarity. You will see how having "too much" limits creativity and innovation. These essays also include timely perspectives on how to deal with the constraint of limited in-person contact through effective digital body language.

Why Creativity Is in Freefall During the Pandemic

By Martin Lindstrom, *Branding Expert & Consultant*

"Everything you can imagine is real."
 — Pablo Picasso

At 11 p.m., I found myself staring at a Word document on the screen. It was only five words long. Over the last 19 days, I'd massaged, changed, and rewritten those five words hundreds of times. Not enough words, for sure, to impress my editor.

Inc. wrote recently that creativity is thriving in these times of COVID-19. In contrast, I think exactly the opposite. Creativity is collapsing in this coronavirus-beset world.

This first dawned on me when I spoke with a friend of mine, the global chief marketing officer of Burger King, Fernando Machado, known for the Andy Warhol primetime Superbowl commercial, the KFC campaign, and the "moldy Whopper" concept. He told me that nearly everyone he knows in the creative field is at a breaking point. Most members of creative teams, he told me, see psychologists on a regular basis. They're simply losing their creativity.

In a time when travel is a memory, long-winded meetings at the office have disappeared, and we have more time than ever at home, why is creativity taking a plunge?

Nearly three decades ago, while working with LEGO®, I conducted a highly unusual experiment, not only to understand creativity, but also to understand how those "new things" (Donkey Kong handheld gaming devices) were impacting kids' creativity. LEGO's destiny was in play, so to speak, as it witnessed its sales being cannibalized by this new global craze. Waving had conducted a similar experiment just a couple of years earlier, but the changes in just two years were astonishing and horrifying. Kids had lost the ability to twirl a pen without dropping it. Simple motor skills were disappearing. And, as kids' play moved from the playground to the screen, creativity had drained from pre-teens' brains.

As time went by, working with creative teams across the world, I noticed that in certain situations, creativity actually seemed to thrive on-screen. But in other situations, it seemed like someone had pressed a writer's block button.

Thoroughly intrigued, I began mapping my own creativity levels, the good days along with the bad, creative moments and the "not so very much," my predictable patterns of ups and downs. It turned out that my most creative moments didn't happen while I was sitting down at a desk, and certainly not while I was staring into a screen. Rather, they occurred in a weightless environment, where the effects of gravity were negligible: in the pool. Transferring this observation into the real world wasn't a straightforward task, of course. For one thing, how was I supposed to take notes while swimming laps? How could I ignore the perplexed stares of my fellow swimmers?

But I did discover that I was able to solve challenging problems in the water, draft that difficult-to-phrase letter, and brainstorm baffling concepts. I could tackle these challenges on dry land, but I'm sure I wouldn't bring the same level of creative elegance to them. I discovered I wasn't alone in this. When I shared my "water moment" insight with other creative types over a late-night drink, they shared with me, half-disbelieving and half-wondering, that they'd come to exactly the same self-realization.

As my thinking evolved, so did my obsession with rescuing my creative mind. I learned that certain types of screen-based interactions not only killed creativity in an instant, but also had a prolonged negative impact for hours after I'd switched off the screen. As I plotted out my lows and highs, a consistent pattern emerged. It surprised me, to say the least. The ultimate creativity killer? My phone.

Most people would argue that the phone has become an essential tool of survival. It's an extended hand, occupying our thoughts and putting our brains on overdrive — even while sometimes paralyzing our minds. I wondered: Could that tool, containing the answer to every imaginable question, offering every source of inspiration, really represent the death of creativity?

On January 1, 2017, I switched off my phone, as a one-man experiment into the phone's impact on creativity. I meant the experiment to last for just one year.

Along the way, I gained some profound insight (and, almost nearly four years later, I still haven't turned my phone back on).

I started seeing things in ways I'd never done before, I rediscovered the joys of silence, and I began meeting new people. In those old days, whenever I found myself at a momentary loose end, I pulled out my phone and did something — anything at all — in order to avoid strangers thinking I'm the sort of lonely loser who's been stood up by a date or a business associate.

However, the biggest surprise to me wasn't what I began to see, but what I began to feel. In the old phone-infused days, I would fill every silent moment with "productive screen time." This was the case on the way to the airport, waiting in the airport lounge, while meeting with clients, at dinner, in the bathroom. The last thing I did before turning off the light at bedtime was to switch off my phone, and first thing in the morning, I'd switch it on again.

If I had a spare minute, I justified the pause by hammering off quick, machinegun instructions to my PA, flicking through hundreds of emails, responding to my staff's 500-word-long, carefully crafted emails with five-word replies. I was on a roll, for sure. By the end of these jackhammer sessions, my squeaky-clean inbox would leave me with me a sense of relief and contribution. And then I'd repeat the process, as all 250 people replied to my replies. Without being aware of it, I kept going back to the future, in the best *Groundhog Day* style. Common sense, for sure, didn't prevail.

Only after turning off my phone for a year did I realize I was never bored.

As months went by without my phone, boredom returned — and with it, time for reflection.

It wasn't easy. Sometimes I suffered withdrawal, like an addict in search of his fix. But with nothing to do — just silence — I found myself combining thoughts in new, unusual, unexpected ways. I spotted details I'd never noticed before. I vacuumed inspiration out of my everyday observations in ways unimaginable when YouTube served as my legal smoking break, tempting me the moment boredom threatened. Did I need a quick fix of self-assurance? LinkedIn lent me a helping hand, while squashing the faintest hint of boredom.

What I began to realize was that boredom, in fact, is the foundation for creativity. I hadn't allowed myself a moment's boredom for decades. Now I endured boredom — and I was more creative than ever.

Recently, as screens replaced face-to-face meetings, the semi-obligatory Friday afternoon beer has morphed into a digital phenomenon. The stroll to the meeting room, the watercooler chat, those casual conversations in the canteen over lunch — moments that management considers "unproductive," "lost hours" that finance tries desperately (and unsuccessfully, I might add) to capture on timesheets — all those moments have disappeared. One by one, they've been converted into a never-ending stream of back-to-back Zoom calls. Something unusual has happened. Productivity has soared. Some measures value increased productivity at billions, if not trillions, of dollars. And, simultaneously, creativity has collapsed.

If I pause for more than a few seconds on a call, someone out there in the dark is sure to say, "Martin, your mic must be muted." Those silent moments of reflection have vanished.

Forget about breaks, even to use the toilet. We've become experts at pretending we're still on the call while doing our business. After all, who would dare reveal needing to go in front of 23 stamp-sized images (though you can bet they're all harboring the same secret desire to hit the loo)?

And aren't we all pretending to be giving this meeting our absolute full attention, despite simultaneously hammering away on a PowerPoint presentation for the Zoom call that's scheduled to kick off 20 minutes from now?

One recent day, after ten exhausting hours, I collected my notes from their 11 open Word files, the results of the day's 11 Zoom calls, and threw myself on the couch — only to realize that my genuine, productive work, actually thinking and reflecting, was only now beginning — at 8 p.m.

It was then, in front of a blank Word document, that I recalled the feeling I had more than three years ago when I put my phone on the shelf. Those mini breaks, those thoughtful pauses, those deep breaths had all but vanished. I was still physically present, of course, locked in front of my screen, but it wasn't really me. It was the robotic, autopilot Martin saying "Yeah, I agree with Ivonne." I'd become the "Send me your deck, Dick," the "You're on mute, Mike," the "I have to jump off for another Zoom" Martin.

We've been seduced into thinking that translating our physical life to a digital lifestyle is a linear process. Not so. Those officially unproductive pauses, those stimulating thoughts, those creative connections, those moments benefiting from a carefully created company culture — all have been lost in translation. Yes, sure: A few industries, like the electronic dance music industry, are indeed thriving.

One of the leading DJs, Martin Garrex, recently said, "We've never been more creative than now." His explanation? This creative tidal wave stems from the fact that they aren't on the road with no time to think and reflect. The draining concert tours, the jetlag, and the endless late hours have been replaced by a "normal lifestyle," spiced up with frequent visits to their home studios. Connecting with fellow DJs around the world, they can ideate and compose remotely. But remember, these industries are built on creativity. Their fuel is sound, not back-to-back Zoom meetings, PowerPoint presentations, and Excel files.

Recently I began skipping every second Zoom call. I shut down my PC after half a day in front of the screen, blocked my calendar, and allowed myself to think. I reintroduced thinking time on dry land as well as in the pool. I reduced those 60-minute-long Zoom calls to 50 minutes each, reserving those 10 minutes for a natural break. Once I leave my office, I avoid the screen.

The article you're reading right now is the one that began with those five lonely words on the screen — those five words I'd been struggling with for 19 days. When I began to take time away from my screen, the words came back to me.

I'll let you in on a secret that may surprise you: I'm still alive.

Cutting down on it all didn't cause me to drop dead on the floor. No one noticed that I was less accessible. No one commented that my stamp-sized photo was missing from the mouse trap of calls. What they did notice was that the Martin they once knew for his creativity had surprisingly returned. No one knew why ... and no one bothered to ask, as they were all too busy jumping on their next Zoom call.

Martin Lindstrom is the author of several New York Times bestselling books that have sold millions of copies and been translated into 60 languages. TIME magazine recognized him as one of the world's most influential people, and in 2020, Thinkers50 named him the #18 management thinker in the world. Lindstrom's latest book, "The Ministry of Common Sense: How to eliminate bureaucratic red tape, bad excuses, and corporate BS."

www.MartinLindstrom.com/CommonSense

How Remote Work Taught Us the Power of Good Digital Body Language

By Erica Dhawan, *Business Growth Coach | Author*

"Remote work is this incredible invitation to really get good at building inclusive cultures where there's a wide variety of types of people, and to build a culture where everyone feels included and everyone is experiencing ongoing growth and development on a regular basis. That's the challenge, and it's not an easy one. But the business isn't easy."
— Shane Metcalf, 15Five

No linguist could have predicted that today, the majority of our communication would happen virtually, even though before quarantine and the rise of remote everything over the last year, digital interaction in all areas of life was slowly but surely becoming a new normal.

With the mass transition to remote work over the past year, many of us have discovered the luxuries—and limitations—of communicating with our colleagues digitally. And while we might have embraced elements of remote work, many of us have also struggled to navigate the nuances and the constraints of an even more digital world.

When the internet came along, no one was ever given an instruction manual for how to communicate in a digitized world. Sure, we all grew up knowing how to read and write, some of us better than others, but there's never been an instruction manual about how to read signals and cues in a digitized world. Instead, so many of us have found ourselves squandering hours or even days at our jobs in uncertainty, anxiety, and disquiet.

And naturally, this shift in how we communicate and work together has bred rampant misunderstandings. Even with emojis and video call options, the loss of the nonverbal body signals and cues that we've been conditioned to employ ourselves and interpret from others is among the most prevalent explanations for employee disengagement.

This issue was illustrated by a meeting I had with a client, a senior leader at Johnson & Johnson who I'll call Kelsey, who had gotten some tough feedback from her team on morale issues. In Kelsey's performance review, her boss commented that her "empathy was weak." When Kelsey and I first met and began talking, I kept my eye out for the standard, universal markers of subpar empathy: an inability to understand the needs of others, a lack of proficiency in reading and using body language, poor listening skills, a failure to ask deep questions.

But Kelsey seemed to have fantastic empathy skills. She made me feel at ease, her body language signaled respect and understanding, and she listened deeply and carefully. What was going on?

The answer had less to do with Kelsey and more to do with today's tech-reliant workplace. Instead of lacking empathy, Kelsey, like nearly everyone I counseled, didn't know what empathy meant anymore in a world where digital communication had made once-clear signals, cues, and norms almost unintelligible. A tone of voice? Approachable body language? Those things didn't cut it anymore. The digital world required a new kind of body language. The problem was that no one could agree on what even made up that kind of body language.

For example, Kelsey believed she was doing everyone a favor by keeping her emails brief. But her team found them cold and ambiguous. Kelsey sent calendar invites at the last minute with no explanation, which made her teammates feel disrespected, as though Kelsey's schedule mattered more than theirs. During strategy presentations, Kelsey would glance down repeatedly at her phone, making others feel like she had checked out.

Kelsey's digital body language, then, was abysmal. It canceled out the very real clarity that comes when workplace colleagues (okay, humans in general) feel connected to one another via physical body language.

So how can we re-establish genuine trust and connection, no matter our distance? Practicing good digital body language.

Communicating what we really mean today requires that we understand today's signals and cues at a granular level while developing a heightened sensitivity to words, nuance, subtext, humor, and punctuation, things we mostly think of as the field of operations for professional writers.

One of the basics of strong digital body language—which surely many of us have learned from our time as remote workers—is the importance of reading carefully and writing clearly. Let's break down what this looks like in practice:

Brevity: Don't Rush to Provide an Answer!

Brevity can make a person appear important, but it can also hurt your business. Sloppy texts and sloppier emails, poor sentences, bad grammar, atrocious spelling—the thoughtfulness (or lack thereof) of a written message communicates a great deal. And while brevity from the upper echelons of power especially isn't exactly uncommon, it's not a great habit to normalize going forward. Getting a slapdash email means that the recipient has to spend time deciphering what it means, causing delays, and potentially leading to costly mistakes. More than that, it can make us come across as insincere and disrespectful.

Be Tone-Deft, not Tone-Deaf

Tone—the overall attitude, or character, of a message—is paramount to good digital reading and writing skills. Perhaps more than anything else, it's the greatest tool for communicating empathy. So, ask yourself: "Who is the recipient? Who is the audience?"

It's no surprise that responding to someone's hard work with a one-word (or one-letter) response communicates a lack of empathy for the person at the receiving end. Don't respond for the sake of responding if you don't have something substantive to offer. If you are having one of those days where you can't give thoughtful attention to an email, send a quick reply acknowledging you received it, and let them know that you plan to respond to it at greater length as soon as possible.

Responding Clearly Shows Empathy and Respect

One of the more obvious reasons our reading skills decline at work is that we're often moving at lightning speed, which makes detail easy to brush over. The thing is, this costs us: Our speed, and the anxiety that surrounds it, erodes our commitment to accuracy, clarity, and respect.

The solution is simple: Proofread your emails before sending them. Take advantage of spellcheck and other proofreading programs. Proofreading is both a habit and a skill: Making it a point of pride to send clean, unambiguous copy will help people take what you write more seriously.

The loss of face-to-face interaction this past year has been a challenge in more ways than one. Beyond the remote office, it showed us how vital cues like eye contact, tone of voice, or body language to clarify what another person means makes digital communication challenging. In lieu of traditional body language, having the skills to read and write carefully is essential to organizations that want to make sure their teams are on the same page and excel in our virtual world.

Erica Dhawan is a leading expert on 21st century teamwork and communication. She is an award-winning keynote speaker and the author of the new Wall Street Journal Bestselling book "Digital Body Language." Download her free guide to End Digital Burnout.

https://www.linkedin.com/in/ericadhawan/

How a Specifically Engineered Values Structure Empowers Us to Prevail in Chaos

By Garry Ridge, *CEO and Chairman, at WD-40 Company*

"Pleasure in the job puts perfection in the work."
— Aristotle

Whatever the external circumstances surrounding our business (pandemic, global political upheaval, a rapidly changing marketplace, or even just an ordinary weekday), leadership is about making tough choices. I would think that everyone would agree with me on that truism. But I'd also like to add that the way you organize your thinking about those tough choices reveals the way you relate to not only your company's values, but also to the way you prioritize them hierarchically as each new tough challenge demands fresh thinking. It is a rare leadership-level decision that has a guaranteed outcome, of course. But what is a guaranteed outcome is that the way we actively use our corporate values as a sort of constraining structure helps us improve our chances of making the best decision available to us. And it breathes life into our corporate culture and protects our relationship with our people – our tribe, as we say here at WD-40 Company.

This is especially the case when the external circumstances are so chaotic – like the COVID-19 pandemic, for instance – that a company and all the individuals associated with it are asking themselves, "Who am I now in the context of this new cataclysmic shift? And how must I change to be most relevant to the times without abandoning my fundamental nature?" To answer these questions, we are wise to go back to that list of what we hold most dear – our values.

It's not enough to simply have a set of values disconnected from each other, with no supporting description of how those values are manifest through actions and decisions. They must be organized – constrained, as it were – according to a hierarchy so that no valuable consideration is skipped over. Nothing is overlooked.

Nothing is sacrificed – even unconsciously and well-meaningly – because individual biases overrule the discipline of the values structure. Let your values set drive your decision-making process in a hierarchical framework, and you remove time- and energy-wasting friction in your corporate culture. And you will build trust among your tribe.

Let me show you what I mean. When I speak to university business classes, I challenge them with a case study exercise that pits competing values against each other: the "right thing to do" for the business, for employees, or for management self-interest. In one proposed solution, the short-term financial returns on the risk have higher odds of being realized than longer-term scenarios.

After the class members receive the case study, I divide them into three groups. Group A gets to tackle the problem any way they want to. Total freedom. Group B must address the case study governed by the set of company values. Otherwise, they're free to strive for the solution to the case study any way they choose. Group C can also do whatever they want, but they are constrained by not only the values but also the values as they are addressed in a hierarchical system. Think of it as them pushing the problem through sieves of ever-finer mesh. Or smoothing out a wooden table using graduated grains of sandpaper.

Because this is my class, I get to decide what the values are and in what order. Naturally, I choose to use the WD-40 Company values in this order of hierarchy (this is just a brief extract; you can read the full description here: https://wd40company.com/our-tribe/our-values/).

We value doing the right thing. We do the right thing in serving our tribe mates, our stockholders, our customers, our products' consumers, our suppliers, and even our competitors — doing what's right according to the situation and the context. If we are honest, and if we speak and act congruently, we will be doing what is right.

We value creating positive lasting memories in all our relationships. As a result of our interactions with our tribe and stakeholders, we all will feel better at the end of the interaction than we did when we began; we will leave with a positive memory of it.

We value making it better than it is today. We strive for continual improvement. There is a special moment that occurs right at the point in time where a person gains an insight or new knowledge because of a particularly positive...or negative...event. We are constantly on the lookout for these "learning moments," because they are the fuel for continual improvement.

We value succeeding as a tribe while excelling as individuals. We recognize that the collective success comes first. Individual excellence is the means by which our organization succeeds. And "excellence" is defined as outstanding contribution to the whole.

We value owning it and passionately acting on it. We get our shoes dirty. We are relentless about understanding our business and our role in impacting it.

We value sustaining the WD-40 Company economy. We exist to create and protect economic value for all our tribe and stakeholders.

After I equip my students with not only these values but also a thorough understanding of how these values are expressed in action and behaviors, I send them off into their three groups to figure out a solution to the case study. By the time their allotted 20 minutes are up, the first group (the one with all the freedom) has come up with only frustration and sometimes even rancor among them. They have experienced what I call "ultimate churn." The second group (the one with values but no hierarchical structure) spent their 20 minutes arguing over which values are most important to serve first.

The third group, however, always delivers its solution first, happy as a group with the conclusion they've come to and satisfied with the outcome.

What does this repeatable experiment tell us? In an organization where you don't have a hierarchical set of values, you get wasted time, friction, and futility. You build dissent among your people, trust is destroyed, and people take offense at a personal level. Subcultures defined by shared points of view begin to form. And these subcultures are like the antibodies that invade the petri dish of corporate culture to devour the good qualities.

Values – along with their hierarchical structure – are the constraints that free us to turn our attention, energies, and synergies to the activities that matter the most to us in the long run. They keep our culture secure and supported while we extend ourselves into unknown variables, territories, and innovations that will take us into a prosperous future. Some might consider them too binding to foster creativity, but I would like to put to you these five ways they free us to do our best work:

Values free us from churn – When we think of churn, we think of lack of direction, a lot of energy invested in going around in circles (consider a washing machine or an ocean whirlpool). There is a lot of yanking about, with no clear exit point where escape can be had. As we have already discussed, churn compromises relationships and trust inside teams (not to mention all stakeholders who have a relationship with your company). Churn stops the free-flowing exchange of information because people begin to prioritize protecting themselves and their careers over the concerns and priorities of their teams and the company as a whole. Your people spend their energies and creative capacity on their self-interest instead of pursuing a solid, unified direction as indicated by your organization.

Values free us from regret – Not every tough leadership decision turns out the way we want it to. That's just a fact of life. But if we are able to "show our work," so to speak, where we can demonstrate how we made our decisions according to the hierarchical structure of the pre-established values set, we can confidently stand by our efforts and say that we did our best. We can transform the disappointment into an extremely valuable learning moment, which will serve us as an entire tribe well into the future. The real gift of the learning moment is that it is an accelerator of the business success; it's a learning moment that we don't have to waste time repeating as a tribe.

Values free us to attract the tribe members we want in our organization – When you can clearly articulate what is most important to your company and culture, and set up your values in such a way that your candidates can see their own values reflected in what you stand for, your selection, recruiting, and onboarding conversations reinforce and reassure all parties that they are in good company. WD-40 Company's employee opinion surveys report that 97% of our people believe their values align with the company's values. And 98% say that they are proud to say that they work for WD-40 Company. When you have that level of alignment, your interactions inside your company culture are richer, free from fear and avoidable discord.

Values free us to attract the right customers – In recent decades, we have come to appreciate the power of inviting our customers to engage with us on levels that are more emotionally evocative than simply choosing a can of oil. We stand for creating positive, lasting memories. Those memories manifest not only in the stories our customers bring to us (repairing a bike for a child, for instance), but they also show up in the message we send to our customers. They belong, for example, to a tribe whose values require a healthy product, manufactured in an environmentally and socially responsible way throughout the world. We belong to each other – company, tribe, customer. And the ground we stand on is enriched by our shared values and the stories we tell each other about how we express those values every day.

Conclusion

In a values-run company culture, the pleasure in the job, as Aristotle put it, comes when our tribe members come to work every day feeling happy to be there, trusting their fellow tribe members, knowing that they will be supported in all they do, inside a circle of safety. They are proud of their work to bring to the world a product that makes a positive, lasting difference in the lives of their customers. They go home at night satisfied that their best talents continue to be invested in an effort to make the world a better place. And they can count on the fact that the next day will bring more of the same: a working environment where they can trust, be trusted, celebrate, and be celebrated, come what may.

When people ask me to help them understand what makes the WD-40 Company culture so successful, I introduce them to this simple formula:

Culture = (values + behavior) x consistency

All those variables and the result of a rewarding culture depend on a deep loyalty to the quality of our individual interactions and decision-making processes in service of our company and fellow tribe members. Other companies may create a list of feel-good values that are easily expressed on company walls, posters, and a page on their websites. And that's all well and good.

But we at WD-40 Company have learned that by creating a values set that truly resonates with authenticity and specificity and by placing them inside a hierarchical structure, we are unleashed to do the thing that prevails over all else – to create positive and lasting memories. Family by family. Household by household. All around the world.

Garry O. Ridge is Chairman and CEO of WD-40 Company. He is also an adjunct professor at the University of San Diego where he teaches corporate culture in the Master of Science in Executive Leadership program. Passionate about the learning and empowering organizational culture he has helped establish at WD-40 Company, he also co-authored Helping People Win at Work: A Business Philosophy Called "Don't Mark My Paper, Help Me Get an A" with Kenneth Blanchard.

https://www.linkedin.com/in/garryridge/

The Beauty and the Beast
Constraints are the Doorknobs to Opportunities

By Mo Kasti, *Founder CEO CTI Leadership and VHS Inc.*

"Those who are skilled in combat do not become angered, those who are skilled at winning do not become afraid. Thus the wise win before they fight, while the ignorant fight to win."
– Zhuge Laing

When my son Adam was two years old, he was dealing with constraints as challenges to overcome. When starting to walk, he would fall but then would stand up and try again. When he realized that doorknobs are essential to opening the door to get to the pool by himself, he figured out how to turn them, so we had to add a lock out of his reach to keep him inside. However, that did not stop him. After Adam realized that he was too short to reach the new constraint, he figured out that he could push the chair to the door, climb on the chair, and unlock the door. He did not see any constraints in the lock. He did not have any assessment of the risk of falling in the pool and thus had no fear of consequences to limit his actions. He did not know what constraints were!

Adam's story is an illustration of how constraints are nothing but a mental model of assumptions and beliefs we make up or develop over time and that are reinforced with data and experiences. One way to illustrate how our assumptions and beliefs impact decision-making and actions is the Ladder of Inference.

Initially developed by Chris Argyris, organizational psychologist and former professor at Harvard, and elaborated on by Peter Senge in *The Fifth Discipline*, the Ladder of Inference is a framework used to describe the way we interpret data and construct meaning. It illustrates how unconscious assumptions and beliefs can drive what data we pay attention to, how we assign meaning to what we observe, and how we see a situation as either a constraint to fall victim to or a challenge to our ambition to overcome.

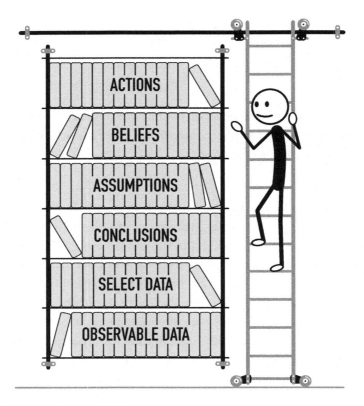

Constraint as Challenge to Ambition to Overcome

I grew up during the Lebanese civil war. As I look back now, I think war is the ultimate constraint generator. Every day, when fighting raged in the streets, damage and dwindled resources followed. In addition to the lack of safety, there was no electricity, no water, no heating and cooking gas, no bread and other essentials. We used to stand for hours in line waiting for our share of bread and then end up baking our own if the bread ran out before getting our turn in line. We also used to wait in line for hours to get drinking water while watching over our shoulders for gunmen or snipers targeting us. Every time a constraint was introduced (by taking away something), I watched my parents and my family try to figure out something else. When there was no electricity, we used to light candles and gas-powered lights until we acquired a small generator. We used to do our homework by candlelight, and the teachers would never accept our excuses that the dog ate our homework, or there was fighting down the street last night.

Constraints made us more resilient and innovative. They made us more determined to excel in school and get better grades, so we could create a better life for ourselves and our family. While it is easy to fall into despair during war, optimism was engrained in us by our families. No matter what happened, our parents were always optimistic that we, the children, would have a better life in the future.

Constraints made me determined to apply for an exclusive scholarship to come to the United States to escape the war. From among 3,000 applicants, and after many challenging assessments, only three applicants received the scholarship to the U.S., and I was one of them. Looking back, if there had been no constraints, probably I would not have become who I am today. I would not have fought hard to get a scholarship and leave the country I grew up in and leave my entire family behind. If it were not for the daily constraints, I would not have landed at the age of 18 by myself in Cleveland, Ohio, at around midnight with two suitcases and only $1,000 in my pocket. If it were not for all these constraints, I would have applied to colleges in my country, like any other student.

Instead, I studied hard, worked tirelessly, finished my undergraduate and graduate schools in four years, and worked in hospitals while studying. If it were not for all these constraints, I would not have become the passionate and the top healthcare leadership coach I am today. War-induced constraints made me innovative and entrepreneurial, willing to take more risks! Because of war, we learned that as long as a risk is not life and death, then go for it.

While constraints have a negative connotation, they are also necessary for many successes and innovation. Constraints can be a stimulus for positive change, and we can use them to arrive at better ideas, solutions, and outcomes.

COVID-19 Constraints Made us More Innovative in Healthcare

In healthcare, where I spend most of my time, we recently faced an unprecedented constraint with COVID-19, which exposed the breakdowns of limited ICU beds, limited ventilators, and limited PPE (Personal Protection Equipment).

These limitations forced us all to shelter at home, so that healthcare resources were not stretched beyond their capacity. But we witnessed innovation and resilience happening. For PPE, we figured out that it was safe to reuse and sterilize N95 masks, while previously we assumed it was a single-use disposable product. As to ventilator shortages, we realized that even a car or a vacuum company can retool to manufacture ventilators.

In the UK, Dyson, which makes suction pumps every day, worked around the clock and developed an entirely new ventilator in 30 days. The company spent around £20m on this project, and Mr. Dyson himself funded this endeavor without accepting any public money. His team worked 24/7 to design and manufacture a sophisticated ventilator in a very short timeframe. In the United States, Ford worked with 3M and GE Healthcare to produce medical equipment including ventilators and protective gear. GM and Tesla have also helped make ventilators. Constraints are the door for opportunities and innovation.

Telehealth was another successful outcome of the COVID constraint. For many years, I have been advocating for the use of telehealth as a more efficient and consumer-centric service to easily diagnose ailments like flu or sore throats. Adoption was very slow, as providers were waiting for insurance and government entities to reimburse them for the time spent. When patients were not able to see their physicians, telehealth adoption skyrocketed. Insurance and government approved its reimbursement (makes you wonder why they did not do that before). For example, Children's Hospital in Wisconsin went from an average of 10 visits per day to 350 visits per day via telehealth. Parents and providers liked it, as it was the only option at the time, and because they realized the possibilities of technology in televisits. If it were not for the COVID constraint, I believe we would not be using telehealth in healthcare.

Constraints are the Doorknobs to Opportunities

In our company, CTI, we saw our training and coaching business come to a screeching halt because of the pandemic. As our healthcare clients got busy with COVID, they cancelled and put all training engagements on hold. This new constraint would have been a kiss of death to any business. Instead, we rallied the team to go virtual and dedicated our time to support our healthcare providers and heroes. We created a website to celebrate the stories of healthcare heroes (thehealthcareheroes.com). We were fully transparent with our team on where we were and how we were handling the new realities that the pandemic was creating for us.

This approach unleashed the team's support for our healthcare clients. We offered our training materials for free with a series of podcasts and webinars focused on wellbeing, communication during stress and crisis, and leadership during crisis. We also offered all our coaching free to any healthcare leader or physician who needed it. The constraint created by the pandemic was the doorknob to new opportunities as it forced us to get into new domains. We moved our yearlong academies from onsite to online (our work is very interactive and experiential), and we moved our coaching and strategy consulting to online. I never thought I could do strategy via Zoom!

Without Constraints, 90% of Organizations Fail in Executing Their Strategy

The statistics of failures in strategy execution are tremendous. More than 90% of organizations fail to execute their strategies successfully (source *The Strategy-Focused Organization* – Robert S. Kaplan and David P. Norton – 2001–2015).

When I work with organizations and leaders on their strategy development, alignment, and execution, I intentionally introduce constraints. To ensure team alignment in strategy and execution, we need to have boundaries and guardrails on the what and how we will use our precious resources of talents, time, and energy. With limited resources, we need to be selective and make hard decisions on what to work on and not to work on. We need to create NOT TO DO lists as much as we need TO DO lists. Using a method and tool called the CTI Line of Sight, I coach boards, executive teams, and leaders to narrow their focus to five areas max to achieve the desired vision and goals.

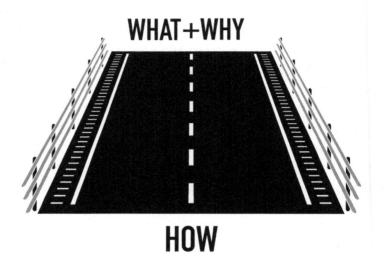

Usually, people have a hard time limiting their focus to five imperatives as they feel it is constraining and may take away from other opportunities. They tend to see it as a beast, not a beauty. I ask them to treat imperatives as guardrails on the highway. You can still select which lane you like to drive on, which speed you like to travel at, and when to switch a lane, but you need alignment of efforts to have the added effect on collective efforts of the whole team and organization.

To accomplish that, I have them do an exercise on how having fewer resources means more innovation and creativity. I ask them to write down 20 items needed to design and open a restaurant. Then I ask them to delete items 1, 3, 5, 7, 9, 20 from the list and try to figure out how they will open a restaurant with what is left on their lists. The teams usually become very innovative and think of creative ways like changing the model to a truck food (when they lost the building item), or bringing your own ingredients to cook at the restaurant (when they lost supplies), or cooking your own food (when they lost the chef in the elimination process). Through this activity, leaders get to see that constraints are very helpful, even necessary, for organizations and leaders to succeed. Limiting our attention to a vital few projects using the Line of Sight tool allows our teams to focus and execute more effectively.

How to Overcome or Leverage Constraints

Here are my ten steps to overcoming or leveraging constraints:

1. See beauty in constraints, not just the beast in them –
Shift your mental model to be able to see constraints not just as a limiting factor but also as the door for more opportunities for growth and resilience.

2. **Connect with your ambition and passion** – Connect constraints to your ambition and passion. Be optimistic that there is always a way forward in any constraining situation. Don't fall victim to a constraint; use it instead as energy for transformation.

3. **Have a clear line of sight** – Realize that sometimes we need constraints to focus our resources and energy, and to have a clear Line of Sight to deliver better results.

4. **Seek other points of view** – Allow others to help you by bringing their perspectives and points of view. Realize that when we are living and working in one curve or paradigm, we don't see the other curve. We need other people's help to be able to see other paradigms.

5. **Be a minus self** – A person that is a positive self (I know it all, I don't need help) tends to repel positive offers of help, as in physics a positive charge repels another positive charge. Be willing to become a minus self, a person who has the humility to accept help from others. Minus self and positive offers of help attract.

6. **Suspend assumptions and beliefs even if temporarily** – This is the hardest step. Suspending assumptions and beliefs, even if temporarily, impacts our identity and who we are. Practice learning how to come down from your Ladder of Inference.

7. **Listen without judgment** – Truly listen to other people's experiences and perspective and say thank you.

8. **Ask different questions** – Think like an artist. Artists don't look at situations as problems. When they walk into constraints like constrained resources, they don't say, "Oops, I have a problem." Instead they ask, "What can I do with what I have? What if?" And as they start their piece of art, they adjust and iterate until they come up with their masterpiece.

9. **Plussing** – Walt Disney coined the term "plussing" as a way of making an idea even better. Telling his workers to plus it, even when they think they nailed it, gave Disney that extra edge when

it came to quality animation back in the day. Pixar is a staunch believer in plussing its work, and it shows in the quality of the work in animations such as *Toy Story 4*. Fifteen of Pixar's films are also among the 50 highest-grossing animated films of all time. How do you build on an idea even if you think it is perfect?

10. **Have the courage to try** – Be willing to experiment and to try new things. Focus on the start, not on outcomes. Just taking the first step to change a constraint is a win. So instead of brainstorming, you need to try-storming. Just try something. You can always go back.

Mo is an entrepreneur, CEO, author, coach, speaker, healthcare catalyst, family man, and average soccer player. Mo's purpose is to transform healthcare by inspiring others to lead with heart, purpose, courage, and uncommon thinking, and harnessing the power of "Us" to deliver exceptional health outcomes. Mo is the founder of multiple healthcare training and service organizations. He is also the author of two Healthcare Leadership books: "Physician Leadership" and "Beyond Physician Engagement." www.ctileadership.com

Mo lives in Tampa, Florida, with his wife Rana and two young leaders, Adam and Jude.

https://www.linkedin.com/in/mkasti/

Sewing Opportunity from the Threads of Adversity

By Michael Canic, PhD, *President at Making Strategy Happen*

"Nothing so concentrates the mind as the sight of the gallows."
— Samuel Johnson

"There are going to be a lot of upset quilters if they can't get their fabric. Not to mention the quilt shops. Many of them could be in big trouble."

Everyone on the TrendTex leadership team nodded their heads. As the leading distributor of quilting and sewing products across Canada, they knew that the government's just-announced COVID-related lockdown was potentially devastating. And trouble for the quilt shops meant trouble for them.

As their strategic consultant and advisor, I had worked with the leadership team to institute the structure and discipline of a strategic management system — a rigorous approach to assessing, developing, and executing strategy. We had achieved impressive results. But now, the dramatic shift in the strategic landscape called for fresh thinking and rapid action. This was a time for quick-cycle strategy.

The challenge was how to keep fabric flowing to the consumer even though the quilt shops were closing down. Many of these shops were small businesses in small towns that relied entirely on in-store sales. Their customers were mostly longtime customers with whom they had built relationships, and who enjoyed coming in to chat while they browsed, examined, and ultimately purchased fabric.

Our first thought was, "How can we help the quilt shops? Could we help them develop e-commerce platforms?" But we quickly realized it wasn't feasible given the number of shops, the varying sophistication of their websites (for those that even had one), and the time and cost required to get them up-and-running.

Could we ship directly to consumers on behalf of the quilt shop retailers? Yes, but how would those consumers be able to check out various fabrics and designs, and how would they place their orders if the shops were closed down?

We explored a number of options yet, invariably found ourselves at a dead-end.

And then ...

"What if the consumers bought directly from us?" Silence.

All of us knew what that meant. We're a wholesale distributor. Our customers are the retailers. If we go directly to our customers' customers, then we immediately become a competitor to them. Not good.

The head of Sales and Marketing immediately said what all of us were thinking.

"We'll lose the trust of our quilt shop customers overnight. The relationships we've built over the years will go out the window. The sales reps will go ballistic."

Right. It made no sense to sacrifice the core of our business, the relationships we had established, and our brand equity, all in pursuit of direct sales to consumers.

More silence.

"What if," one team member then asked, "there was some way we could make this a win for our customers as well as the consumers? What would that look like?"

"Well," said another, "whatever we do to help consumers can't in any way compromise the customer relationships."

That was the refresh we needed. Now we went to work. We reexamined our business model with that core requirement in mind: Protect the retailer and help the consumer. We asked what our customers needed, facing an impending lockdown. They needed timely access to the high-quality fabrics and designs they had come to expect, and sufficient variety to meet their customers' needs. And with so much uncertainty on the horizon, they didn't need the costs and challenges associated with buying and receiving inventory, or being stuck with untimely or unsold inventory. Finally, they needed to get paid. What did their customers need? Sufficient variety and timely delivery of the fabrics they wanted. Period.

The challenge was to design a model to best meet those needs. What resulted was the *TrendTex Partnership Program*. We designed a dedicated website — a digital showroom of fabrics — to give consumers simple and easy access to our extensive selection of fabrics and designs. However, to make a purchase, at checkout they had to enter a code provided by, and unique to, one of our quilt shop customers. If they hadn't received or couldn't find their code, they could simply select the name of their preferred quilt shop from a drop-down menu. No code or no shop name meant no purchase. That ensured our quilt shop customers got credit for every purchase. In fact, they received the same financial credit as they would have if the consumer had purchased in-store. The program provided a natural incentive for our quilt shop customers to promote their unique codes. The more they promoted their respective codes, the more they sold.

Of course, the right messaging was critical. Our good intentions could have been misinterpreted and perceived as a threat if we weren't completely transparent in explaining all aspects of the program. Talking points were developed to support real-time customer calls. Simple and intuitive marketing collateral was created to give our customers a quick and easy guide to the program.

What happened? Not just the proverbial win-win, but a win-win-win. Many of our quilt shop customers saw the program as a lifeline to keep their businesses running. As a result, they vigorously promoted their unique codes to their customers. Their customers responded favorably. They appreciated the quick and easy access to the high-quality fabrics and designs they wanted, and the convenience of having them delivered to their homes. For TrendTex, the Partnership Program was a major success. In addition to the sales generated, helping our customers in a time of massive uncertainty strengthened relationships and deepened loyalty. That ultimately led to a strong increase in our wholesale sales as well.

The Takeaways

Four key takeaways emerged that speak to having the right mindset and taking the right actions:

1. **Embrace strategic agility** – While it's important to establish a regular cycle for strategy development, it's equally important to trigger real-time strategy when the environment changes and the situation dictates.

2. **Reframe difficulty as opportunity** – As a wholesale distributor, it would have been easy to view ourselves as a helpless victim of the drastic changes taking place in the retail environment. Yet by reframing the situation as a problem to be solved, we were able to design a solution.

3. **Be sensitive to the ecosystem** – Don't jump at immediate opportunity. We could have met consumers' short-term needs by bypassing the retailers and selling directly to them. But that would have caused irreparable damage to our core business. See the big picture. Consider the implications of your actions for all key stakeholders.

4. **Meticulously manage messaging** – With the retailers already anxious because of the pending lockdown, sending the wrong messages could have heightened their fears and undermined our program. Messaging can make or break your efforts. Be sure to think through the details of what to communicate to whom, how, and when.

With any adversity come opportunities. With the right mindset, you can discover them. Through the right actions, you can fulfill them.

Michael Canic is the President of Making Strategy Happen, a consulting firm that works with committed leaders to turn strategy into reality. He has delivered more than 600 presentations on four continents and is also the author of the bestselling book, "Ruthless Consistency: How Committed Leaders Execute Strategy, Implement Change, and Build Organizations That Win."

Michael@MakingStrategyHappen.com

Prioritizing Projects to Remove Implementation Constraints

By Antonio Nieto-Rodriguez, *World Champion Projects and Project Management*

"The bad news is nothing lasts forever. The good news is nothing lasts forever."
— J. Cole

P rioritizing is usually seen as a personal skill and a way of addressing constraints. You prioritize when you look at how you are spending your time today, this week, this month, or this year. But, prioritizing is also a key organizational capability. Indeed, understanding how and why organizations prioritize their activities and their time constraints is vital to their success. Yet, surprisingly, this is one of the least understood and most neglected areas of organizational life.

The word priority appears in the English language as early as the fourteenth century. The Merriam-Webster dictionary defines it as "what matters most." In the UK, priority is used to describe which vehicle has the right to go first at a road junction. In organizational terms, prioritization sets the agenda in terms of what really matters, which is reflected in how resources are allocated – especially the scarce resources of time and money.

I have over 20 years as senior executive prioritizing, selecting, and managing projects, including time and resources constraints, within large corporations. In my experience, one of the main reasons that many companies fail is due to a lack of a clear sense of what is urgent or simply selecting the wrong priorities. Get your organizational priorities wrong and the effects can be calamitous.

Look at two classic corporate failures of recent times. Think of Kodak. It wasn't that it didn't foresee the rise of digital photography, but it chose to prioritize the wrong things. In the 1990s, Kodak invested billions of dollars into developing technology for taking photographs using mobile phones and other digital devices. But in a classic case of Clay Christensen's innovator's dilemma, it held back from developing digital cameras for the mass market because it feared that would kill its all-important film business. Meanwhile, the Japanese company Canon recognized the strategic priority presented by digital photography and rushed in.

Similarly, the Finnish company Nokia developed the technology for smart phones earlier than most of its competitors, yet it decided not to launch projects in this field and instead prioritized exploiting existing products. If it had chosen different priorities, Nokia could still be one of the leading telecom operators in the world.

If the executive team doesn't prioritize, middle management and employees will, based on what they think is best for the organization. At first, we can think that this a good practice; empowering people to make decisions is something that we have all heard since the time of Peter Drucker. What organization doesn't apply it? Yet, without having a prioritized set of strategic objectives, the consequences are often disastrous.

To illustrate this, let's look at the following real example. Sam worked as a teller in a local bank serving customers. He loved his job, and his father had also spent his entire career in the same bank, but like many other banks, the company was struggling to survive due to low interest rates, increased competition, and the burden of cumbersome regulations. The executive team worked months to identify a new strategy that would help to turn around the company, identifying two strategic priorities that they believed would secure the company's future.

In a series of town hall meetings, the CEO informed the staff, Sam included, that the new strategy of the bank was based on two strategic priorities: improve the customer experience: increase satisfaction by 20%; increase efficiency: serve 20% more customers per day. The message was crystal clear: As long as Sam and his colleagues kept focused and met the two strategic priorities, the company's future and their jobs were assured.

The day after, Sam was extra motivated after hearing his CEO saying that it was in his hands to safeguard the company he cared so much about. He kept the two strategic objectives in mind and started to serve customers as efficiently as possible, always with a smile. That worked fine until a customer started to talk about a personal loss and the terrible situation he was going through. He clearly wanted to talk with Sam, who was initially pleased with the idea as it would significantly increase customer satisfaction. However, after a few seconds, he froze.

What about the second strategic objective, efficiency? If he spent a few minutes talking with his customer, his client-servicing rate would suffer. What was he meant to do? He didn't know which objective was more important, but it was his decision. And the problem is that all the bank tellers were facing the same dilemma every day.

The executive team thought that they had clearly communicated the strategic objectives to turn around the bank, but in fact they had created an operational dilemma. The bank didn't improve performance, and many employees who loved their jobs and worked hard to implement the new strategy were fired.

A well-communicated sense of organizational priorities helps to align most of the projects and programs in an organization to its strategies. This alignment is often championed by business thinkers. But, the reality of an organization is much more complex than many suggest. Sometimes the strategic objectives are not clear, or are nonexistent. Often there is a gap and lack of alignment between the corporate strategic objectives and the ones from the different business units, departments, or functions.

What I have learned is that for an organization to prioritize effectively, it has to recognize and articulate what really matters first. I tried to apply the theories and tools available in the market, yet none proved to be successful. They miss pragmatism, require inputs that would take months to collect, and would need a large team to keep up to date.

To address the challenges of prioritization that I have been confronted by over my career as an executive in several multinationals, I developed a simple framework that I call the "Hierarchy of Purpose."

Both the Board of Directors and the Executive team can use the tool to rank priorities and select strategic initiatives.

Purpose – Vision and Mission are often mixed up, and their differences are not understood. Therefore, they are hardly ever used when strategic objectives are set, and the staff doesn't know what really matters. Use purpose instead. State the purpose of your organization and the strategic vision supporting this purpose. The purpose has to be sharp and clearly understood by anyone working for your organization. Amazon's purpose "to be earth's most customer-centric company" is so compelling that it will avoid any ambiguity within the organization.

Priorities – The number of priorities admitted to by an organization is revealing. If the risk appetite of the executive team is low, the team will tend to have a large number of priorities; they don't want to take the risk of not having the latest technology, missing a market opportunity, and so forth. On the other hand, if the executives are risk takers, they tend to have a laser-like focus on a small number of priorities. They know what matters today and tomorrow. Define the priorities that matter most to your organization now and in the future. Take the example of Amazon, whose purpose clearly puts the customer in the center. As opposed to Sam at the bank, everyone working at Amazon will know when they have to make decisions, the ones related to customers will always go first.

Projects – Strategic initiatives and projects, when successfully executed, bring the organization closer to its purpose and its strategic vision. Nowadays, companies have a large number of projects running in parallel, mostly because it is easier to start projects than to finish them. Very often, capacity, and not strategy, determines the launch of projects. If people are available, the project is launched. If not, it is just dismissed. Who wants to risk missing a big opportunity? But which projects should organizations really invest in and focus on?

By using the answers to the first two points of the hierarchy of purpose, senior executives are able to identify which strategic initiatives and projects align best with the purpose, vision, and priorities. It also helps to identify those that should be stopped or scrapped. Although theorists suggest developing formulas that automate the process of prioritizing and selecting ideas, my recommendation is not to use such a systematic approach. The exercise is mainly to provide management with different orientations and viewpoints, but the ultimate decision has to be made by management based on human intelligence.

People – Prioritizing at an organizational level is incredibly difficult. Large organizations are made up of individuals with their own strong sense of what matters. Every individual in an organization has their own list of priorities. These are by their nature self-serving, informed as much by personal ambition and aspiration as any sense of alignment with the organization's strategy. Yet, as shown in the example with Sam, employees are the ones implementing the company strategies. They perform the day-to-day business activities and deliver the projects. They also have to make many minor decisions and trade-offs every day. Creating clarity around the priorities and the strategic projects of the organization will make sure that every employee works in the same direction. It is important that you allocate the best resources to the most strategic projects and that you liberate them from day-to-day operational tasks: Projects are delivered more successfully when they have a fully dedicated team and a strong, committed, and proactive sponsor.

Performance – Traditionally, performance indicators don't measure priorities and seldom indicate the progress according to implementing a company's strategy. Project metrics tend to measure inputs (scope, cost, time) instead of outputs. Inputs are much easier to track than outputs (such as benefits, impact, and goals). Identify indicators linked to the organization's priorities and to the outcomes expected from the strategic projects. Less is more in this case, so one or two for each area will do the job. It is better if people remember by heart how performance is measured. The ultimate goal is to have the few outcome performance indicators embedded in people's minds. Finally, management should have the right information to quickly react to market changes and to supervise the pipeline of new priorities.

Among the organizations I have worked with – and others such as Apple, Amazon, Lego, Ikea, and Western Union, which all have highly developed senses of priorities – the payoffs of using the Hierarchy of Purpose are considerable: They can experience significant reductions in costs as priority activities that fail to deliver against clearly articulated measures are stopped, and there is potential to reduce duplications, consolidate activities, and decrease budget overruns. Overall, prioritizing increases the success rates of the most strategic projects, increases the alignment and focus of senior management teams around strategic priorities, and most important, creates an execution mindset and culture.

One of the main hidden benefits I have seen every time I carry out the first round of prioritization with top management is that the discussion turns into a very interesting strategic dialogue. For example, the CEO might ask the director of sales, "How are we going to meet that international growth target if currently we only invest in existing markets, or compliance takes up to 60 percent of our project capacity? Is this sustainable in the long term? What would be the consequences of balancing our portfolio and investing more in growth and cost optimization, and less in compliance?"

Think of your organization's purpose and priorities.

Are all of your employees working according to those priorities?

Are the activities prioritized in the best interests of the organization as a whole?

How would your priorities change in case of a sudden economic downturn?

Antonio Nieto-Rodriguez *(antonionietorodriguez.com) is a leading international authority in project management, strategy implementation, and leadership change. He is considered the World Champion of Project Management and* *recognized by Thinkers50 with the award "Ideas into Practice." Antonio is the author of "Lead Successful Projects" (Penguin, 2019), "The Project Revolution" (LID, 2019), and "The Focused Organization" (Taylor & Francis Group, 2014), and is currently writing on the "Harvard Business Review Project Management Handbook" (HBR, 2021).*

https://antonionietorodriguez.com/

No Money, No Problem!

By Rob Nail, *Advisor, Mentor, and Developer at Hammerfx | Former CEO at Singularity University*

"For me it was never about money, but solving problems for the future of humanity."
— Elon Musk, entrepreneur

As an entrepreneur, one of the most important lessons learned is that "cash is king." Usually this refers to managing your money intelligently so that you don't run out. But there is a much more nuanced cash-constraint equation that can unlock continuous innovation at any company or project.

A typical excuse and constant complaint I hear in most projects and many startups is that they don't have enough money to do what they want. Money is always an easy excuse for not being able to do something, but the real hurdle is almost always with mindset.

Constraining capital (and time) can be a great forcing function for a lean startup mentality in any project and will almost always result in new options and unexpected innovations.

In my first startup, Velocity11, a few friends and I bootstrapped a robotics business to automate drug discovery and cancer research. As you can imagine, building high-end robotics for the biggest Pharma and biotech companies requires significant capital. Unfortunately, in 1999, at the height of the Dotcom boom, the last thing any investor wanted to put capital into was a hardware company. You could raise almost a hundred million dollars for a pet food website, but a company with a patent portfolio, product prototypes, and early-development partners was toxic. We probably should have built a website instead, but we were passionate about the work we were doing and the potential we had to help scientists with their work to cure some of the diseases that plague humanity. So, we racked up debt on credit cards and asked friends for favors.

I have never been as committed and hard-working as when all of my money was on the line, and for a time, I even gave up my rent and started sleeping under my desk at the office. Now, there is a fine line here where going too far leads to bad decision making out of personal fear or worse, impacting the security of a family. But as with any constraint, you will never know how much you can do until you test the limit directly.

Fortunately for us, this level of commitment and frugality forced us to think creatively in almost every aspect of what we were doing. One of the biggest breakthroughs was innovating our sales process such that we were selling "customized solutions" for our customers and were able to command 40% payments upfront. In reality, we largely built the same thing for everyone, but made some aesthetic and software tweaks to make it seem tailored for each application. This was a big software breakthrough in the industry at the time, but for us, the 40% payment innovation covered all of our costs for the projects and allowed us to grow to profitability and beyond without millions of dollars of investment capital.

We also innovated the product-development phase and integrated the customers throughout. This is where I learned that an expensive "sales team" may be the last department to invest in. Having a sales person as the interface to the customer, interpreting for the organization, can be a catastrophic mistake. Instead, thinking of everyone in the company as a "sales person" creates amazing new opportunities for innovation and authenticity. A company's purpose is ultimately to deliver value to its customers, and every employee in the company should see how their role is helping deliver that value. As we experienced many times, a random watercooler conversation between a visiting customer and any employee can turn into a transformational selling moment. A customer will always trust these authentic interactions far more than some high-priced sales person's pitch.

As companies grow and scale, there is also an ever-present risk of allowing bureaucracy to slip in and that clarity of value proposition to blur. Every investment in the company, whether hiring people, adding software tools, or purchasing supplies, should have a clear contribution to its value proposition. Maintaining a disciplined mindset focused on value is a difficult constraint, but it will keep the company from losing its way and its customers.

Through the companies I have started and run as well as various projects I have overseen, I believe there is a strongly skewed bell curve relationship between capital and innovation.

The Innovation Capital Curve

In a few cases, having zero capital doesn't work, since you need some number of supplies and resources to run experiments and launch new products. But in most cases, very little capital is actually needed to develop, test, and launch a product today. We are now in the age of free research tools, free design tools, free collaboration tools, and open-source tools and code sets for almost every feature you could imagine. For a few dollars, you can harness the power of virtually unlimited super-computer computation in the cloud. Even the cost of starting a new business today is only a few hundred dollars and can be done in an afternoon.

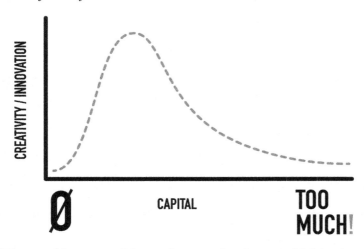

What could you possibly need money for that would drive innovation? Well, maybe coffee, but beyond that, money has very little to do with innovation. In fact, it often gets in the way as we get lost trying to find ways to spend it.

Forget about the money. Set that aside for another day and focus on solving the problem at hand without it. Spend time and energy understanding the customer need at its most granular level and see what it takes to solve just that.

At Singularity University (SU), I had the great pleasure and challenge of running a rapidly growing startup that achieved a scale and level of expectation that I had never experienced before.

In the beginning of SU, a small group of thought leaders came together with the insight that technology is progressing far faster than most people believe and should be used as a tool to solve problems that were never believed possible to solve – what we called the Global Grand Challenges. As a startup, there was very little money to spend on high-end displays or graphics or all the things we expect today from a leading high-tech institution. Instead, the faculty found creative ways to deliver an immersive experience that was life-changing and sparked thousands of creative new ideas to solve the world's biggest problems, all without spending much money.

Field trips to see the first Google car, pool sessions to explore weightlessness for future space-related challenges, and role-playing exercises to explore the various ethical challenges of technologies today were just a few of the transformational elements that students experienced. It was this base of innovation that launched an extraordinary business and movement in the world.

Having been the CEO through much of its growth journey, it's painful to reflect back on this lesson as it is now so obvious. But at the time, the growth and success were quickly followed by significant capital and bigger expectations – to the point that nothing short of a product launch with "everything and the kitchen sink" was going to be perceived as a success. The money got in the way of our mindset.

It quickly becomes far easier to "throw some money at it" when pressured to go in new directions. Investing in many different initiatives and paths may appear like a lot of innovation is happening, but it can be misleading as it can be very capital-inefficient. For us, time was prioritized over money, and we began paying external consultants to do work that we didn't have time to do. Our initial digital course launch fell victim to this growth-trap mentality. We assumed that by putting more money into the projects, we could overcome the failings. But in hindsight, instead of trying to roll out a whole suite of new courses on a new education platform with badging mechanics and collaboration tools baked in, we should have launched smaller elements far sooner and made traction with our core customers.

It's not uncommon for companies to make the error of waiting too long to put a product out into the market, but perfect is always the enemy of the good. When it comes to product launches, my favorite guiding quote is from Reid Hoffman, the founder of LinkedIn: "If you are not embarrassed by the first version of your product, you've launched too late." Setting a time and capital constraints are usually the quickest ways of getting engineers to come up with creative solutions and to say "It's done!"

One area where we actually succeeded was with the expansion of our global chapters. Instead of funding these "properly" to copy and scale our business, we starved them to success. We provided small steps towards successful growth and allowed each chapter to find its own path from there. What resulted was a level of creativity and collaboration that we could never have expected. New variants of our programs and events were being tested at a record pace, and those successes and failures were being shared organically within the network. Because there was a tremendous opportunity, but with limited capital, the innovation was forced to blossom.

Of course, in success and with growth, you will have to add capital to keep up the momentum. However, having too much money early on is a growth trap that often leads companies away from their strengths and isn't sustainable – just ask where WeWork is today. Once the creative spark is lit and a growth engine is started, maintaining the momentum while keeping the innovation hot requires a delicate balance on the capital throttle.

In order to maintain a lean startup mentality, one exercise we developed at SU was the "pre-mortem" exercise. As part of any development project, spend some time imagining what would happen in the future if you had too much money. Can you imagine a future scenario where having too much money would lead to failure? Write down the details of those scenarios and let them guide risk-mitigation strategies for future product launches.

Don't get me wrong: Having more money than you could need is a great problem to have – but it is still a problem. The more common problem, of course, is thinking you need money to move forward. In fact, it is precisely when we need money the most that our most creative and innovative selves can arrive. Don't let money get in the way of innovation. Let it affect your balance sheet, but not your mindset. Stay hungry and focused on the customer value proposition, and you can break through the capital constraints of your innovation process.

Rob is an Associate Founder and former CEO of Singularity University and currently works as an Advisor, Mentor, and Coach, and is exploring A.I. with his webcast "Robot & Rob." He is also a serial entrepreneur, engineer, investor, director, surfer, and a struggling homeschooler, but mostly, a proud husband and father.

His personal mission is to build bridges to an amazing future.

www.robnail.com

How Career Constraints Can Build Stronger Employee Motivation

By Adrian Gostick and Chester Elton, *New York Times Bestselling Authors of Anxiety at Work and Leading with Gratitude; Founders of FindMojo.com*

"It's not what you achieve, it's what you overcome. That's what defines your career."
— Carlton Fisk

Years ago, we worked for an executive who was wont to say as we handed him assignments: "This isn't it yet, but I'll know it when I see it." He thought he was giving "creative freedom" that would encourage our best work; in reality, he was ratcheting up anxiety levels to excruciating levels.

How were we supposed to know what he wanted?

The fact is, constraints, limits, and restrictions provide direction in all aspects of our work. And after two decades coaching executives—and having surveyed hundreds of thousands of employees for our books—we can attest that a good deal of employee anxiety comes from a lack of constraints in how people are managed. Much of the rising anxiety levels we see in employees today comes from a lack of clarity about their own performance and growth opportunities.

There are two simple things most people want to know at work: "How am I doing?" and "Do I have a future here?" We've found most managers, however, create more ambiguity than clarity around these ideas because they are loath to set any limits on people.

Of course, there are formal methods of giving employees feedback, e.g., the annual review, but research has shown these infrequent check-ins are woefully inadequate at addressing the uncertainty that many feel about their jobs in the six or twelve months between these meetings. In fact, many progressive firms have decided to abandon performance reviews entirely, replacing them with other processes for evaluating and developing employees that are more timely, frequent, and concrete. We call this process of putting positive constraints on the performance of team members the continuous review, a way of supplying ongoing feedback and gauging employee performance with real-time metrics.

It makes sense: Since childhood, we have been raised to judge ourselves through a continuous review. As school children, we knew our work would be judged by letter grades that came almost daily. If we did poorly on one quiz or test, there was always another to come. These continuous reviews at school created an environment of lower risk, higher feedback.

Then we got to the workplace, where we abruptly entered an environment of infrequent, higher-risk reviews that proved to be extremely anxiety-inducing.

Greg Piper, worldwide director of continuous improvement for Becton, Dickinson & Co., holds one-to-one performance and development sessions every other week for thirty minutes with each of his team members, who are all remote and spread around the globe. " 'What do you want to talk about?' is always the first question I ask," Piper told us.

Since Piper's meetings with his team are so frequent, letting his people guide the discussions is an especially effective way to get real-time information about their challenges and success. He's then able to be more clear in his direction, set constraints, and prioritize work.

Stephan Vincent, senior director of LifeGuides, a peer-to-peer support network, says he begins his check-in sessions by gauging how his team members are coping. "My first message to everyone on my team is, 'How are you feeling today?' Because today is probably different than yesterday."

He explained that these check-ins before diving in should not be rushed, and people should have time to tell their stories if they want to share. It's up to a leader to dig below the "fine." This is one manager who is creating a more personal connection with his team, which makes them more open to hearing constraints or limitations since they know he has their best interests in mind.

"The workplace of tomorrow will be much more human, and less transactional than it's been," Vincent added. "As we create deeper bonds, it's ultimately going to benefit the company with more productivity, more collaboration, more innovation."

Evidence on the value of concrete, frequent check-ins comes from BetterWorks research, which found employees who meet and discuss progress toward goals with their managers weekly are up to twenty-four times more likely to achieve their targets. By providing such constant reviews, managers are also able to give tough feedback when necessary and quell anxious feelings in many employees who are doing good work but are actually concerned about their performance.

According to a Leadership IQ survey of thirty thousand people, only 29 percent of working adults know whether their "performance is where is should be." Just as troubling, more than half say they rarely know if they are doing a good job.

Tyler, a customer service employee we met, said he began to feel adrift after moving from a highly communicative manager who often gave constructive feedback to a new boss who was more tight-lipped. Not knowing what this new boss thought about his performance, or if he felt he could progress any further in the company, Tyler finally pushed the boss for some feedback to lessen the uncertainty he was feeling. They sat down and the manager delivered some positives he had seen to date and also gave some things to work on. The big message Tyler took away: There actually were constraints on his growth, and Tyler admitted that he found that "jarring." He ended up obsessing over the negatives the boss outlined. He's not alone.

The human brain has a negative bias. There is a greater surge in electrical activity in our brains in response to negative news than upbeat. When we hear negative things about ourselves, it sticks like Velcro to our memories—even if the good outweighs the bad by ten to one. Ironically, that may have been why this manager was so loath to give feedback to any of his people in the first place. "Who wants constraints on their careers, right?" thought this manager.

Tyler allowed us to coach him to try something new when the pair met again. We told him to first pay attention to any and all positives the boss was saying and write them down. We told him not to focus on any improvement ideas until he had captured all the manager's thinking on his good attributes. He reported back that it felt remarkably weird taking notes on the good stuff his boss was saying, and even odder to ask for clarifications on those positives; but after just ten minutes of this, he began to realize that his manager was well aware of his strengths.

Tyler then saw the improvement ideas his boss was offering in a new light. Yes, he was being told there were constraints on his growth—he needed new skills and experience before he could progress—but the manager was offering Tyler honest and helpful ideas to help him develop his talents. Tyler realized the coaching was not an indictment of his abilities overall. The constraints to his career were realistic, and he left the meeting with newfound confidence that he could work within them to grow and develop.

We find that even though most people are more than capable of going beyond what is asked of them, modifying their behavior to hit new goals, or growing to be able to tackle new responsibilities, many never do more than is asked since leaders don't clearly talk about career constraints and opportunities. Many managers want their people to believe that the sky is the limit, when what people really want is a realistic path.

Realistic clarity about performance and career growth from managers in one-to-one settings gives workers a sense of what's achievable and what may not be achievable given the current circumstances. It also helps people understand what kind of actions are necessary in the moment. Clarity like this helps employees take on new projects or oversee tasks, because they understand the parameters of their new responsibilities and what freedoms in decision-making they have.

Adrian Gostick and *Chester Elton* are #1 bestselling leadership authors and organizational culture expert. Gostick and Elton are authors of "All In," "Leading with Gratitude," and "Anxiety at Work," all New York Times bestsellers. They work with organizations around the world to address employee engagement and leadership development issues.

www.adrian-gostick.com and www.chesterelton.com

Bright Future

"My personal war cry is, 'Bright Future.'"
— Frances Hesselbein

By now you have learned insights from Marshal Goldsmith's 100 Coaches on how to turn obstacles into opportunities. What you do with this new-found knowledge is up to you. In this section, Marshall Goldsmith, the world's #1 Executive Coach, shares what he is doing with our shared ultimate constraint: Time. You will benefit from design-inspired thoughts on how constraints can inspire creativity to inspire you and how looking to the future may inform how you are today.

Gift From the Future?

By Dr. Tasha Eurich, *Organizational Psychologist, New York Times Bestselling Author ("Insight," "Bankable Leadership")*

"A prudent question is one-half of wisdom."
  – Francis Bacon

A s an executive coach—and aggressively curious person—I am a lifelong fan of prudent questions. In my coaching work with C-level executives, I have seen time and again how they provoke insights that are both illuminating and unexpected.

Good questions are like grease in the gears of self-awareness.

Personally, I can trace one of my most life-changing insights to a question I was asked by a mentor and dear friend, Marshall Goldsmith. It was July of 2020, and the COVID-19 pandemic was raging.

Marshall and our mutual friend Mark Thompson had recently invited me to participate in their new project, the "Life Plan Review" (or LPR). They had chosen a diverse collection of 50 powerful participants: high-profile CEOs, influential government and nonprofit leaders, famous athletes and performers, brilliant bestselling authors, and more. Every weekend, we got together on a Zoom call to review our progress on our personal and professional goals.

Given the vast accomplishments of my fellow LPR members, I sometimes felt a bit of imposter syndrome, especially given what I'd been experiencing in the preceding few months.

Up until the pandemic, though few people would describe me as relaxed, I'd been proud of my grit. No matter what life threw at me, I had always managed to stay functional, even hopeful, through difficult times.

But March of 2020 changed all our lives, overnight and forever. For me, my life as a global speaker and consultant came to a screeching halt.

And after spending 20 years building this career I loved so deeply, I was rudderless. If I wasn't running through airports, sitting in boardrooms coaching CEOs, and on stage delivering keynotes, suddenly I had no idea who I was.

I also knew that others had lost much, much more than I had, and that the best anyone can do is to try and keep going. I did my best to stay on a path that resembled the one I was on before (virtual keynotes and coaching, starting a new book, etc.), but it felt futile. I began to wonder how, or even whether, I'd be able to exist in this new, forever-changed reality. On a good day, I felt exhausted. On a bad day, it was hard to even go through the motions.

So during our LPR call with Marshall and Mark that July morning, I took my laptop out to the deck of my apartment and reported my progress to the group—forcing a smile and trying to find a positive spin, even though I felt like I was drowning.

When all the report-outs were finished, Marshall announced he had an important question to ask us:

"Imagine that it's one year from today. The 'future you' is thanking the 'current you' for a gift that helped them enormously. What gift did the current you give the future you?"

The question took my breath away.

If the "before times Tasha" had been on that call, her answer would have been, "My gift to the future me is a finished book proposal." But not that day. Before I could even put my answer into words, I felt an immense sense of relief.

Fighting back tears, I willed Marshall not to call on me, which of course, he did.

After a deep breath, I revealed, "This is really hard to say out loud... but I think the future me is going to thank the present me for sticking around. For having faith that life wouldn't be this way forever...and for not giving up."

I couldn't believe what I'd just said, and immediately starting crying—not just crying...ugly crying—which, in front of so many famous people, is exactly as embarrassing as it sounds (though, unsurprisingly, in the many messages of support I received after that call, I discovered that I wasn't the only person experiencing this).

And the clarity I finally felt that day made it worth it. My answer to Marshall's question gave me one of my most important insights about myself. I'm fairly certain that it saved my life.

I discovered that I needed to immediately reprioritize my life, at least for the time being. The best thing I could do for the future me was not, in fact, to keep throwing myself into my work. It was to finally get help, so I could find the energy to keep fighting. (Incidentally, this theme of "not giving up" is powerfully embedded in the many inspiring and instructive the stories throughout this book.)

This question has since become a touchstone for me in times of challenge and crisis for one powerful reason: Imagining ourselves one year into the future provides a roadmap for what our present self needs most urgently.

How would you answer Marshall's question? Think of the biggest challenge you're facing as you read this: What gift will the future you thank the present you for? Is it to focus on what matters most? To let go of something? To stop doing what's no longer serving you? (The preceding essays have surely offered several additional ideas!)

Because, as I discovered, the answer might be different than you'd expect. But even if you don't have an immediate answer, that's okay. Just sitting with the question will be powerful. After all, as Rainer Maria Rilke aptly observed in *Letters to a Young Poet*, we must "live the questions now. Perhaps then, someday far into the future, you will gradually, without even noticing it, live your way into the answer."

Dr. Tasha Eurich is an organizational psychologist, researcher, and New York Times bestselling author. Globally recognized as the #1 self-awareness coach and organizational culture expert, she applies the principles of behavioral science to help leaders achieve dramatic and measurable change. Her TEDx talks have been viewed more than 8 million times, and famed Wharton professor Adam Grant calls her most recent book, "Insight," one of the three books he recommends most often.

www.Tashaeurich.com

Constraints Are the Heart of Creativity

By Ayse Birsel, *Co-founder of Birsel + Seck and Author of Design the Life You Love*

"Here is one of the few effective keys to the design problem—the ability of the designer to recognize as many of the constraints as possible—his willingness and enthusiasm for working within these constraints. Constraints of price, of size, of strength, of balance, of surface, of time and so forth."
— Charles Eames

We all have constraints. What can set you apart from others is the willingness and enthusiasm described by Eames. If you can have the optimism to see constraints as opportunities, you will create new value.

This is creativity.

Get into the habit of shifting a constraint into an opportunity. The more you practice this with everyday limitations, the better you will be at seeing things from multiple directions.

That small apartment you've been complaining about is easy to clean. Your long commute is precious alone time to read, to listen to music, or to play games. The travels that take you away from family are also your opportunity to meet new people, to try new food, and to sleep without your children waking you up.

Think like Pollyanna, the children's book character, who sees difficulties in life cheerfully, to hone your skill in flipping constraints to opportunities.

Use existing constraints as the building block for your next solution. Francis Mallmann, the three-star Argentinian chef, is famous for cooking in the Patagonian wilderness. His constraint? No kitchen. His opportunity? To invent new cooking and barbecuing techniques. His experiment is well-documented in the Netflix series *Chef's Table*.

Charles and Ray Eames used the limits of plywood to invent new furniture. Their constraint was single-shell plywood chairs, where the back and seat were made of one continuous piece that cracked. Their solution, through trial and error, was to design plywood chairs made of two pieces, a separate back and seat. They joined the two pieces with an additional plywood spine, or on another design, with a metal frame. The Eames lounge chair, recliner, etc., are all variations on this theme.

Julia Child created *Mastering the Art of French Cooking* in response to constraints. At the time, Americans didn't have French ingredients, and they valued practicality and speed over taste. Child rewrote French recipes with American ingredients and modernized them to be simple and accessible to Americans. Another constraint she had was that the French learned how to cook from their parents. She became the surrogate mother and taught the process on TV.

Elon Musk didn't have the money other established car companies had when he started his company, Tesla. That was his constraint. He turned it into an opportunity by creating a pre-order system where he painted a picture of the future for his buyers and convinced them to pay for their cars in advance. The preorders funded and continue to fund an important part of Tesla's development costs.

Work with your constraints, not against them. Make someone else's constraint your opportunity.

The constraint of the traditional taxi service model was that the customer had to go to the service, rain or shine, rush hour or not. Uber took that constraint, which everyone knew existed but hadn't solved, and created a model where the service goes to the customer, when they need it, where they need it. Uber's willingness to tackle a constraint that others took for granted is what made that business unique.

Is there a glaring constraint that none of your competitors are willing to solve? That is your opportunity.

Make constraints your ally. The trick is seeing negative issues as positive opportunities.

Here's how.

Thinking outside of the box may have become a cliché, but that's because we've forgotten what it really signifies. Take a moment to visualize it. Can you see the box? It is defined; it provides boundaries. To think outside of the box, first, the "box" must exist. You need something to push against. In other words, you need your constraints.

Here are examples from serious outside-of-the-box thinkers – Elon Musk, Charles Eames, Issey Miyake – on how to turn constraints into opportunities, the next time you bemoan them.

Define a game-changing constraint

Sometimes a given constraint is so extraordinary that it becomes an incredible game-changer.

If you are reading Elon Musk's biography like I am these days, take note of the many constraints Musk puts in front of his team at SpaceX to arrive at extraordinary solutions that are changing the space industry.

My favorite anecdote is how his team invented a thruster engine out of a mind-boggling single piece of metal (made with a 3-D printer) to outperform anything that is normally manmade in parts and welded together.

Next time you want to think outside of the box and innovate disruptively, define the box in a radical, counter-intuitive and non-traditional way.

Instead of trying to bend the seemingly unbendable, find a way to bend with it

Everything has constraints: materials, processes, people. Work with them.

Charles Eames, the industrial designer, was a master at working with constraints. His ground-breaking work in plywood is a case in point. Imagine what plywood is – layers of thin wood, like a ream of paper. If you take a ream of paper and you want to curve it, you can only do it in one direction. It is the same with plywood; you can only bend it in one plane. That was Eames' constraint and chance to innovate. He realized this and then bent with it. His plywood furniture is a testimony to his genius.

"I have never been forced to accept compromises, but I have willingly accepted constraints." – Charles Eames

Like the Zen master who works with the stones in the Zen garden, work with the stones and make them part of your solution.

Turn annoyance into advantage

When Japanese fashion designer Issey Miyake was asked to design a travel collection in the 1970s, he didn't know that the project would come to define his work. As a first step, he defined his box by asking what happens to your clothes when you pack them. The answer – they wrinkle. That became his key constraint. So how did he push against that? Instead of working against wrinkles, Miyake turned them into intentionally designed pleats and came up with what is now a big part of his brand, Pleats Please. He saw an opportunity in an annoyance and turned it into a world-renowned brand.

So next time you have an annoying constraint, think how you can make it your biggest advantage.

Constrain yourself to one basic criteria

Sometimes the most liberating thing is to be restrained to one medium. Look at Twitter and its 140 characters. Painter Chuck Close's pixel paintings, now a beautiful part of New York's Second Avenue subway. How Sean Kenny creates art using LEGO® blocks. Real Simple's 3-ingredient recipes. Bach's Goldberg Variations, which are 30 variations on one aria. Japanese haiku, poems with only 3 lines, including one of my favorites here:

First autumn morning
the mirror I stare into
shows my father's face.
— Murakami Kijo

Define a singular focus, intentionally limit your resources, and give yourself tunnel vision within which to explore the maximum number of variations, ideas, designs.

Sometimes being constrained is exactly what you need to think without limits.

Maybe because I grew up in the Turkish culture, I am determined to see a silver lining in any situation. I love using constraints as a tool to think differently. How about you? I would love to hear from you about how you think outside of the box and turn constraints into opportunities in your life and at work.

Design the life you love![6]

*Ayse (pronounced Eye-Shay) **Birsel** is one of Fast Company's Most Creative People 2017 and is on the Thinkers50 Radar List of the 30 management thinkers most likely to shape the future of organizations. She is the author of "Design the Life You Love" and gives lectures on Design the Work You Love to corporations. Ayse is the co-founder of Birsel+Seck, the award-winning design and innovation studio, and consults to Amazon, Colgate-Palmolive, Herman Miller, GE, IKEA, The Scan Foundation, Staples, and Toyota, among others. Her work can be found in the permanent collection of the Museum of Modern Art (MoMA).*

https://www.aysebirsel.com/newsletter

---

[6] This chapter is developed from the thinking included in articles that previously appeared on Inc.com.

Dealing with My Ultimate Constraint: Time

By Marshall Goldsmith, *World's #1 Executive Coach and*
New York Times Bestselling Author

"In a curious way, age is simpler than youth, for it has so many fewer options."
— Stanley Kunitz, *Former U.S. poet laureate*

My mission in life is incredibly easy to understand, yet infinitely complex to achieve. My mission is to:
Help you become the person that you want to be – and to help you help others do the same.

Who is the "you" that I am referring to in this mission? Individually, that person is the "you" who is reading this article right now. Collectively, I would like for the "you" to be as many human beings around the world as possible – both now and in the future. While it is very admirable to help unsuccessful people who are in great need and solve their problems, my goal is different. I want to help successful people get even better – so they can help the world.

Helping great people – and especially great leaders – provides exponential leverage. For example, I am not an expert on the environment, but I have coached Mark Tercek, a wonderful environmentalist who led the Nature Conservancy for ten years. I am not an expert on Women in Leadership, but I have supported Sally Helgesen, the world expert on this topic, who has helped thousands of women leaders. I am not an expert on eliminating world poverty, but I have helped Dr. Jim Kim, whose work has helped save millions of lives as the head of the World Bank. I am not an expert on leading organizations that impact millions of people, but I have coached many of the greatest leaders in my lifetime including Alan Mulally (Boeing and Ford), Frances Hesselbein (Girl Scouts USA), Hubert Joly (Best Buy), and Deanna Mulligan (Guardian Life).

In order to best accomplish my mission, I want to have a positive impact on as many people's lives as possible, in the time I have remaining.

My ultimate constraint is time.

At this writing, I have just turned 72. The average male in the U.S. at my age has a life expectancy of about 13 years. On the other hand, that does not mean that the average person will be productively engaged as a professional for all of those years.

Although I am in excellent condition for my age, I am not in denial about aging. Realistically speaking, I will be very fortunate if I have ten more years to make a significant positive contribution to the world.

My wonderful friend, Whitney Johnson, has been consistently ranked as one of the *Thinkers50* Most-Influential Management Thinkers. Whitney has taught me a valuable lesson. Our constraints are our motivators!

I see my limited amount of time as highly motivating. I have a lot to do – and not that much time to do it. While I am not going to help everyone, I want to help as many people as I can! To best achieve my mission, I need to keep moving forward as rapidly as possible. As Whitney so wisely puts it, my constraint is my inspiration!

I will share four key elements of my plan for the rest of my life and illustrate the importance of my key constraint – time.

100 Coaches – After being inspired by Ayse Birsel, one the world's experts on *Design the Life that You Love*, I decided to "adopt" 15 people and teach them all that I know at no charge. The only expectation was that they "pay-it-forward" and do the same for others. I posted a primitive 30-second video on LinkedIn asking if anyone was interested in being one of my "honorary children." I thought that maybe 100 people would apply and that I would pick 15. I was wrong! So far, over 18,000 people have applied, and we have about 300 members (although the program is still named *100 Coaches*).

Our members include an amazing array of some of the world's most accomplished people including many of the Thinkers50 top management thinkers, several million-plus-selling authors, all of the *Thinkers50* Most Influential Coaches in the World, for-profit and not-for-profit CEOs, Hall of Fame athletes, Broadway stars, TV journalists, leading professionals from many walks of life, as well as fascinating younger people who are embarking on their careers.

My goal is to involve as many great professionals as I can in 100 Coaches in my few remaining years. My wish is for many of these great people to replicate this process by "adopting" their own "pay-it-forward" families. Tasha Eurich, *The New York Times* bestselling author of *Insight*, has already begun this process by "adopting" ten wonderful humanitarians in the "Tasha Ten." Dr. Raj Shah, President of the Rockefeller Foundation, is following her lead in choosing ten "Game Changers" who are focused on global development. Alisa Cohn, the leading coach for startups, has selected great people for the 100 Coaches, who have then "adopted" more people. We are now in our fourth generation!

I now have an official nonprofit organization to support this cause, the *100 Coaches – Pay-It-Forward Foundation*. My hope is that ultimately this project will have a positive impact on thousands of people around the world. Although my personal constraint is time, my hope is that this process will live on beyond my lifetime.

Knowledge Philanthropy – The *Knowledge Philanthropy* (KP) Project represents a very different way to consider the dissemination of intellectual property. Traditionally, if anyone wanted to use another person's intellectual property, the user had to use the material as packaged, without any modification. Along with the limitations in interpretations, the user had to pay money to the developer of the intellectual property – or risk being sued for "infringement." The KP approach is exactly the opposite; users can use intellectual property in any way they wish. The ideas can be modified or changed to fit the needs of the audience and no pay is expected from any nonprofit organization. For-profit organizations can pay, only if they wish, and any money collected will be donated to the 100 Coaches Foundation.

I am beginning the KP project with my own content and materials. So far, hundreds of my articles and hundreds of my videos are available online at no charge. Tens of millions of people have read these articles and viewed these videos. I would next like to make all of my material more user-friendly, so it can easily be found on an as-needed basis and help people who speak many different languages.

I would also like to expand the KP idea around the world. For example, Nankhonde Kasonde-van den Broek is one of Africa's leading coaches. She is developing very innovative leadership development training for high-potential leaders across Africa. Nankhonde is including my content in her work and changing it in a way that fits her unique group of leaders. To me, this is a perfect application of our KP philosophy. I am not an expert on high-potential leaders in Africa, but by supporting her, I can indirectly help them. As these leaders become more effective, they can then become a positive influence on countless colleagues across Africa.

My ultimate goal is to expand KP well beyond my personal materials and content. I see myself as a "pilot project." Other great leaders and thinkers will ultimately be able to plug into the systems that are developed for my content and use the same process to disseminate their knowledge to the world.

Back to my ultimate constraint – time. I have a lot of people to reach!

AI Video Bot – I love the concept of having a video bot. The bot will look like me, have my voice, and be programmed with Artificial Intelligence to provide responses and answer questions. While the technology required to produce lifelike and helpful video bots is not quite where it needs to be today, it is getting better and better! Ultimately, I would like the bot to be programmed with my knowledge, but also have knowledge from other thought leaders that I respect (with their approval and support). By using the latest AI technology, my bot will hopefully be able to answer questions from interested learners around the world – in their own language.

The AI Video Bot can be used to support our *Knowledge Philanthropy* project. My vision is for other thought leaders to also have video bots that build upon their great ideas. In that way, concepts can be shared around the world in a very user-friendly format that can be duplicated over the generations.

One of my concerns is that the work of the great teachers who have impacted my life will be lost. For example, Peter Drucker and Warren Bennis have been wonderful teachers and thought leaders who have had a huge positive impact on my work and my life. Although their lifelike video bots may never be available, readers (with permission) could be used to create AI audio bots that could serve a very similar function. Although an interested student in Zambia – 40 years from today – will never be able to have a phone call with Peter Drucker, Peter's audio bot could give her a very similar experience.

Although the challenges in making AI bots a reality are daunting, we have an amazing group of volunteers who are hard at work with the goal of making it happen. This team is being led by Asha Keddy, a brilliant leader and thinker, who is also a top executive and AI expert from Intel.

While I will never see the impact that this project may have fifty years from today, I am very inspired to see how far we can make this go in the time I have available!

Content – While I have developed a large body of content related to helping successful people get even better, I have more left to develop. I am very excited about my next book, *The Earned Life*, which I hope can help millions of people. As a person who has been a philosophical Buddhist for almost 50 years, I would love to write a book on how Buddhist psychology can be used to help leaders and coaches. As a student of Peter Drucker's, I would also like to write a book about how Peter's great work applies to coaches and leaders in our new world.

Back to my Knowledge Philanthropy project. I would love to help some of the great executives that I have met package and deliver their approaches to leadership, so their ideas are accessible to leaders across the globe. One of the best ways for leaders to learn is from other leaders. The KP project can be a very meaningful way for leaders to leave a legacy that impacts other leaders around the world.

Along with developing new content, creating an AI bot, supporting *Knowledge Philanthropy*, and building *100 Coaches* – I still want to coach a few executives, build a new coaching methodology (based partly on the work of Alan Mulally) called the Life Plan Review, stay in good physical condition, and be a good friend and family member!

I have so much to do that I am starting to get tired just reading this chapter! I think that I will go take a nap – but not for too long.

I don't have that much time!

Dr. Marshall Goldsmith *is the only two-time Thinkers50 #1 Leadership Thinker in the World. He has also been recognized as the World's #1 Executive Coach and a Top Ten Business Thinker for eight consecutive years. He is also the #1 New York Times bestselling author of "Triggers," "MOJO," and "What Got You Here Won't Get You There."*

e-contact for Marshall: info@marshallgoldsmith.com

Afterword

Reflections on a Year that Turned Our World Upside Down

John Baldoni, *Globally Recognized Executive Coach, Leadership Educator & Author*

The little boy, just two, stood and stared.
In disbelief.
His look was not of sadness.
It was dismay.
How could you?
You just got here!
Even after he had pulled on his Gee-Ma's coat.
"Off, off", he said. (Meaning stay, stay.)
But she could not.
A fleeting visit, too hurried.
And off she went back into the gloom we call Covid.

+++

What We Endured

It did not happen suddenly.

Reports from Wuhan about a novel corona virus made some news.

When the virus struck Italy, people asked:

"Was this a real-life case of Contagion, the movie about a pandemic emanating from China?"

In short order, the virus spread to Washington, Oregon, California, and New York.

Then it was everywhere.

From March on, the days became a blur.

Blursday as one smart person on Twitter wrote.

Hours dragged into hours.

Minutes clicked. Seconds dragged.

Even digital clocks seemed still.

Wearing and weary, we persisted.

Blursday after Blursday.

Boundaries no more between home and work.

Some made the shift to virtual without missing a step.

Others stumbled, tripped, and fell flat.

Yet time at work, at home, speed up.

Zoom at dawn.

Zoom at noon.

Zoom at dusk.

Zoom, Zoom, Zoom.

I read somewhere that the CEO of Zoom never intended for Zoom to be like this.

Easy for him to say.

Zoom is here to stay.

At work we toiled on screen.

Pivot became our watchword.

Become virtual we said.

Talked to a screen.

Stared at a screen.

Screamed at a screen.

Always on.

Always there.

Was this our new companion, a kind of avatar?

One without warmth. Just a cold stare.

There, there, there.

Kids rootless now.

No school. They, too, on Zoom.

For some it was a breeze. For others a struggle.

For Moms and Dads a relentless push.

Pull. And Push.

To keep them focused. On track. And learning.

Learning? We hoped.

Isolation and disconnection became our norm.

No longer meeting for coffee over break.

Or seeing friends for drinks.

Those residing in a single domicile were the fortunate ones.

Hugs and kisses were still allowed.

Those alone had no such luck.

Just their solitude to keep them company.

I attended a wedding. Via Zoom.

The many gathered virtually, listened intently

As vows were exchanged.

Those present clapped and cheered.

And those far away smiled and some even shed a tear.

United in spirit. Virtually.

Social hour became virtual, too. Virtual cocktails. Virtual dinners.

Virtual, virtual, virtual.

As the joke goes, the only thing worse than being virtual is not being virtual at all. Count your blessings.

You still had your friends.

+++

What We Saw

Our televisions brought our sordid history back to life.

The asphyxiation of George Floyd by a white police officer reminded us again how little some lives do matter.

It was one of many such killings. White cop on unarmed Black civilian.

This time it was different.

We saw it on television. Again. Again and again.

Seemingly non-stop.

People took to the streets to protest.

There was order mostly and some were joined by the police themselves.

Yet there was disorder, too. Looting and destruction.

Something else, though, a footnote perhaps.

So many doing the reporting, the arresting, the adjudicating and the pontificating were themselves Black.

Surely, we were better than our forefathers? Maybe!

We were awakened, as we have been before to the injustice that lies before us.

Social justice cannot be cured with more laws, more protections.

It must come from our sense of "people-hood."

If Covid has taught us one thing, it is that we are all in this together.

White. Black. Brown. Yellow. Red. And every shade in between.

Calling themselves patriots, insurrectionists besieged the U.S. Capitol.

Their presence was an ugly reminder of the divisions that separate us.

Nothing good can occur when people who traffic in violence are allowed to riot.

Covid, too, has given us the opportunity to think, re-think really, who we want to become.

Society must change, we agree.

But no change can occur without a look in the mirror.

The change we seek must come from a reflection on how we think, feel, and act.

Bias is our protection we think.

It shields us from having to think more deeply about the injustice around us.

It's not my problem, our bias tells us. It is "their problem."

Wrong, of course, the mirror does not lie.

+++

What We Lost

Ourselves mostly.

What we imagined for ourselves once no longer seemed so sure.

Once we counted on this and that.

Now we know "this and that" are no more.

We lost our security.

Our illusion of destiny.

A life planned is an illusion, after all.

"Man plans, God laughs" goes the saying.

Never more true than now.

Colleagues have moved on.

Their jobs no more.

We feel sad for them, but secretly breathe relief.

"I am still here."

We lost civility, too.

Those who did not wear masks taunted those who did.

And vice versa.

Meanwhile Covid cases continue to rise by the millions.

We lost friends.

Covid does not play favorites.

The losses mount.

Day after day.

First, we lost as many as were lost on 9/11.

Then all those who were killed in Vietnam.

Next Korea. And World War I and II.

What does it matter to compare?

We lost people.

"An empty chair," our new president reminds us.

I attended a funeral. By Zoom.

The handful of mourners present at graveside

Were dwarfed by the hundreds watching via Zoom.

Less a funeral and more a celebration of life.

Moving all the same.

The loss is there. Felt by all. Even on the Zoom.

+++

What We Gained

Resilience.

We learned we can get knocked down. Hard.

And get back up again.

More vulnerable, more humble now, yes.

And more courageous.

More alive, too.

Resilience is our tool for re-invention.

We become transformed.

The world we left behind is no more.

It is up to us to create what we like to call the "new normal."

We gained also a sense of ourselves.

Who we are as a people.

Friends. Colleagues. Families.

Husbands. Wives.

All brothers and sisters in creating something different.

We do seem altered as a people.

Living with a plague can do that to you.

Yes, we saw vitriol, but we also witnessed more grace. Much more.

We saw neighbor helping neighbor, and strangers helping strangers.

Communities reaching out to those in need.

And lastly there is hope.

Holding us tight as we hold on to it. We feel it.

We embrace it.

We even hope for it.

Hope is like that.

We hope for something better.

To go outside and breathe deeply without fear.

To mingle with others without fear.

To congregate for worship, or for play.
We need hope. It sustains us all.

+++

The boy of two smiles now.
His Gee-Ma has returned.
All vaxed up, coat off and ready to play.
Smiles.
Laughter.
Joy.
We have survived.

John Baldoni *is a globally recognized leadership educator, certified Master Corporate Executive Coach, and author of 15 books that have been translated into ten languages.*

In 2021, the International Federation of Learning and Development named John a World-Class Mentor and named him to its Hall of Fame. Also in 2021, Global Gurus ranked John a Top 20 global leadership expert, a list he has been on since 2007.

www.johnbaldoni.com

Acknowledgements

SPECIAL THANKS to the members of the Marshall Goldsmith 100 Coaches who contributed content for this book and for their advice and encouragement along the path to completing this work. Each of them made a unique and personal contribution and was always available to provide support and insight.

Julie Carrier, John Strelecky and Sarah McArthur, also members of the Marshall Goldsmith 100 Coaches, helped guide the process to create this book through direct contributions of their experience. They each provided just what was needed and did so at exactly the right time.

Family and many friends helped along the way by listening, brainstorming, sharing thoughtful reference materials and providing encouragement. I am especially grateful to my daughters Jamie Verhun and Alexandra Verhun and friends Graydon Hall, Ben Sillem, James Szarko, Melissa Allan and Dr. Michael Naugle.

Without Linda Verhun, Marshall Goldsmith, Scott Osman, Ayse Birsel, Chester Elton, Adrian Gostick, Bill Carrier, Julie Carrier, Erica Dhawan and Mo Kasti this book would never have been possible.

Thank you all.

About Darcy Verhun

DARCY VERHUN is the President of FYidoctors, that has emerged as one of the fastest growing diversified healthcare companies in North America.

Darcy obtained his MBA from the Richard Ivey School of Business at the University of Western Ontario. Prior to joining FYidoctors he held senior leadership roles at Ernst & Young, Grant Thornton and Cap Gemini. Darcy has been recognized as a Fellow of the Chartered Professional Accountants of Canada and also as a Distinguished Alumni of MacEwan University. He is a Certified Corporate Director, Certified Management Consultant and holds a Bachelor of Commerce degree from the University of Alberta.

Darcy was a founding Director of The Calgary Homeless Foundation. He serves today as a Director of HomeSpace Society, a non-profit which is intent on eliminating homelessness. In addition to his commitment to help those in need, from his early days as an aspiring ski racer, he remains a passionate skier and has achieved the highest level of ski instructor certification in Canada as a Level IV.

Darcy lives in Calgary with his wife, Linda and their two daughters, Alexandra and Jamie.

Darcy's leadership is based on being a lifelong learner and passionate coach who lives his life with gratitude. He is known for the high energy and commitment he brings to everything.

Made in the USA
Las Vegas, NV
18 September 2021